Naples and the Amalfi Coast

Withdrawn from Stock

D0716528

0   5 km

0   5 miles

INSIGHT GUIDES

NAPLES

& THE AMALFI COAST

Step by Step

APA PUBLICATIONS L

Part of the Langenscheidt Publishing Group

CONTENTS

Withdrawn from Stock

ABOUT THIS BOOK

This *Step by Step Guide* has been produced by the editors of Insight Guides, whose books have set the standard for visual travel guides since 1970. With top-quality photography and authoritative recommendations, this guidebook brings you the very best of Naples and the Amalfi Coast in a series of 12 tailor-made tours.

WALKS AND TOURS

The tours in the book provide something to suit all budgets, tastes and trip lengths. As well as covering Naples and the Amalfi Coast's many classic attractions, the routes track lesser-known sights and up-and-coming areas; there are also excursions to the key archaeological sites and the bay islands. The tours embrace a range of interests, so whether you are an art fan, a gourmet, a nature lover or have kids to entertain, you will find an option to suit.

We recommend that you read the whole of a tour before setting out. This should help you to familiarise yourself with the route and enable you to plan where to stop for refreshments – options for this are shown in

the 'Food and Drink' boxes, recognisable by the knife-and-fork sign, on most pages.

For our pick of the walks by theme, consult Recommended Tours For... *(see p.6–7)*.

OVERVIEW

The tours are put into context by this introductory section, giving an overview of the city to set the scene, plus background information on food and drink, shopping, entertainment, and sports and outdoor activities. A succinct history timeline highlights the key events that have shaped Naples and the Amalfi Coast over the centuries.

DIRECTORY

Also supporting the tours is a Directory chapter, comprising a user-friendly, clearly organised A–Z of practical information, our pick of where to stay while you are in the city, and select restaurant listings; these eateries complement the more low-key cafés and restaurants that feature within the tours and are intended to offer a wider choice for evening dining.

Above: a dazzling view from Capri's Giardini di Augusto; the ornate interior of the Palazzo Reale; a sun-baked street in Herculaneum; stunning vistas abound from Ischia; Naples' handsome neoclassical Villa Pignatelli.

The Author

Natasha Foges moved to Italy in 2003 for one year and ended up staying for four, during which time she took on an array of jobs, from paparazzo's assistant to Latin teacher, before trying her hand at travel journalism. Now an editor and travel writer based in London, she spends much of her time pining for the southern Italian sunshine, and goes back as often as she can to soak up the atmosphere and tuck into some world-class pizza.

Many of the tours in this book were originally conceived by Italy expert Cathy Muscat.

Margin Tips

Shopping tips, historical facts, handy hints and information on activities help visitors to make the most of their time in Naples and on the Amalfi Coast.

Feature Boxes

Notable topics are highlighted in these special boxes.

Key Facts Box

This box gives details of the distance covered on the tour, plus an estimate of how long it should take. It also states where the route starts and finishes, and gives key travel information such as which days are best to do the route or handy transport tips.

Route Map

Detailed cartography shows the tour clearly plotted with numbered dots. For more detailed mapping, see the pull-out map slotted inside the back cover.

Footers

Look here for the tour name, a map reference and the main attraction on the double page.

Food and Drink

Recommendations of where to stop for refreshment are given in these boxes. The numbers prior to each restaurant/café name link to references in the main text. Restaurants in the Food and Drink boxes are plotted on the maps.

The € signs at the end of each entry reflect the approximate cost of a two-course meal for one, with a glass of house wine. These should be seen as a guide only. Price ranges, also quoted on the inside back flap for easy reference, are:

€€€€	over 40 euros
€€€	26–40 euros
€€	16–25 euros
€	15 euros and below

ANCIENT WONDERS

Tour 6 visits the marvellous archaeological sites of Pompeii and Herculaneum, while a trip to the Campi Flegrei (tour 5) takes in an array of fascinating sights, from a Roman amphitheatre to the mysterious cave of the Cumaean sibyl.

RECOMMENDED TOURS FOR...

ART BUFFS

The churches of Naples' *centro storico* (walk 1) are crammed with Baroque masterpieces, and the modern-art museum is an essential stop; don't miss the Museo di Capodimonte (walk 4), one of Italy's finest art museums.

ESCAPING THE CROWDS

Despite its astonishing sights, the Campi Flegrei area (tour 5) is low on tourists; Capri (tour 10) is heaving during the day, but at night is free of crowds; Procida (walk 12) is a sleepy refuge from the bay's busier sights.

FAMILIES

In Naples, the kid-friendly combination of castle, park and aquarium make walk 3 ideal; the friendly atmosphere of Sorrento (tour 7) and the lovely beaches of Ischia (tour 11) make these a good bet for families.

FOODIES

For genuine Neapolitan pizza, the rowdy *centro storico* (walk 1) is the place, and a fish feast in Borgo Marinaro (tour 2) is a must. The Sorrentine Peninsula (tour 7) has a clutch of gourmet restaurants.

GETTING BACK TO NATURE

The Sorrentine Peninsula (tour 7) is a walker's paradise, while Ischia (tour 11) offers natural hot springs and a picturesque setting. Away from the tourists, Capri (tour 10) has some wonderful walks. For an awesome encounter with Mother Nature, visit Vesuvius (tour 6).

RAINY DAYS

Many of the attractions of Naples' *centro storico* (walk 1) are indoors, while the city's world-class museums (tour 4) hold enough masterpieces to keep you occupied for the best part of a day; or you could hole up in one of Ischia's spas (tour 11).

ROMANTICS

The Amalfi Coast offers romance in spades (tours 8 and 9), while the lack of crowds and the stirring vistas of picture-perfect Procida (walk 12) make it an ideal romantic getaway.

SEASIDE FUN

Positano's beaches (tour 8) are large, with plenty of facilities; the Sorrentine Peninsula (tour 7) has good, tucked-away swimming spots, while Ischia and Procida (tours 11 and 12) boast lovely beaches and crystal-clear water.

STREET LIFE

For a heady dose of the vibrant street life that defines the city, a stroll through Naples' *centro storico* (walk 1) can't be beaten, while the streets of Sorrento (tour 7) and Capri (tour 10) are also always bustling, if somewhat more genteel.

OVERVIEW

An overview of the region's geography, customs and culture, plus illuminating background information on food and drink, shopping, entertainment, sports and outdoor activities, and history.

INTRODUCTION

Disorderly, down-at-heel, rowdy and exhilarating, the capital of the hot-blooded Italian south is like nowhere else. The Bay of Naples holds its own irresistible charms, from dazzling islands to slumbering volcanoes, and from world-class archaeological sites to the sinuous Amalfi Coast.

Population
Naples is the third-largest city in Italy after Milan and Rome, with 963,000 inhabitants; when its crowded and ever-expanding suburbs are included, however, the figure is around 4.5 times bigger than this.

Below: friends outside Caffè Gambrinus (see box, p.37).

Naples lives by its own rules. Utterly lacking in tourist-ready gloss, the city demands that visitors give in to the flow of local life; the noise and chaos may be alarming at first, but a wander through the *centro storico* will soon win you over. All human life is played out here: boys dodge the traffic to play street football; old men cluster on street corners and argue about politics; mopeds bearing entire families buzz down the narrow streets, klaxons blaring; workers cram into tiny bars, putting the world to rights in their coffee break. And those clichés of a bygone, earthier Italy that have all but disappeared elsewhere – glittering shrines, lines of washing and raucous local markets – are everywhere you look in Naples.

At the heart of it all, and visible for miles around, stands Vesuvius, a potent symbol of the beauty and cruelty of nature and a huge influence on the Neapolitan character (*see box, p.12*).

Beyond Naples' suburbs, nature takes over. Seek refuge from the clamorous city along the Amalfi Coast, in the rugged Sorrentine Peninsula and on the islands. There's something for everyone here, whether you're looking for a family break, a romantic getaway or a few days of solo pampering.

GEOGRAPHY AND LAYOUT

The Bay of Naples and Amalfi Coast are part of Campania, one of the four provinces that make up southern Italy. The landscape is volcanic, its topography formed by ancient craters and the deposits left by thousands of years of volcanic activity. The most prominent landmark on the bay is

Vesuvius (1,017m/3,336ft), dormant since its last eruption in 1944 (the only active crater in the region today is the Solfatara in the Campi Flegrei). The southern end of the bay is bounded by the Monti Lattari, a hill range that forms the backbone of the Amalfi Coast.

Naples

Once you get your bearings, Naples is an easy city to navigate, and the main areas of interest to tourists can all be covered on foot. Driving is not a viable option – traffic is solid in the city centre, parking nightmarish and Neapolitan drivers anarchic, to say the least. To travel between city districts, stick to the cheap and easy public-transport system. Buses can be slow, and the metro is undergoing a major overhaul, but the funiculars that ferry people up and down the Vomero hill are ultra-efficient, and the trains and boats in and out of the city are plentiful and smooth-running.

Day Trips from Naples

Naples is a good base for exploring the historic sites in the bay area: trains to the Campi Flegrei, Pompeii and Herculaneum run frequently from the train station at Piazza Garibaldi. The bay area as far as Castellammare di Stabia is built-up, with ugly industrial estates and housing blocks at various stages of disrepair, but between the grim buildings sprout citrus trees

and olive groves, and the sea and mountainous backdrop are constantly magnificent. South of Castellammare, the urban sprawl dwindles away, replaced by a captivating landscape of green hills, plunging cliffs and picture-postcard towns.

Beyond Naples

After a few days exploring the city, you will be craving some calm. The laid-back town of Sorrento is perfectly positioned for exploring the islands, the Amalfi Coast and Pompeii. If you don't want to hire a car and tackle the Amalfi drive yourself, the blue SITA buses run regular services between Sorrento, Positano and Amalfi.

In summer, ferries carry day-trippers from Sorrento and Naples to the islands. But to absorb properly the wild beauty of Capri's coastline

Above from far left: a patriotic young cyclist; detail of the magnificent Galleria Umberto I; the Amalfi Coast is great for quality ceramics.

Above: scenic Amalfi; ancient Pompeii.

Campania Artecard

If you are planning to see quite a few sights during your trip, the Campania Artecard (www.artecard.it) could be a worthwhile investment. Several varieties are available; one particularly useful option is the Napoli e Campi Flegrei card, which gives free access to the first three of many of the key attractions in Naples and the Campi Flegrei, plus half-price entry on all remaining sights, and includes public transport (valid for three days; €16). The three-day Tutta la Regione card (€27) includes even more sights, including Pompeii and Herculaneum. Buy the card online, at participating museums, at tourist offices *(see p.91)* or from the Artecard info-point in the central station.

Language

You won't find English spoken everywhere in Naples, as you do in many other European cities, though staff in hotels and many shops usually speak some English. Italians appreciate foreigners trying to speak their language, even if it's only a few words.

and find time to relax in Ischia's hot springs after sightseeing, consider an overnight stay. Procida is so small that you could easily walk round it in a day, though it is still a pretty, peaceful place to spend the night, and only a short hop from Naples.

HISTORY

For nearly three thousand years, Naples was fought over and occupied by a succession of foreign powers. Greeks, Romans, Normans, Arabs, Angevins, Spanish and Bourbons – all left their mark, not just on the streets and buildings, but on the language, culture and character of the Neapolitans themselves. Gregarious by nature, their clan-based

communities and innate disrespect for authority are rooted in centuries of foreign domination.

Art and Architecture

Naples' chequered history has resulted in a variety of architectural styles, though medieval, Renaissance and Baroque churches, castles and *palazzi* predominate. Much of the art you are likely to see in Naples is in the Baroque style. This was sparked by Caravaggio, who pitched up here in 1606 after the Roman authorities put a price on his head for killing his opponent in a tennis match. A wanted man, he didn't stick around for long, but long enough to paint some of his greatest paintings and influence a new generation of artists

Superstitious Naples

Naples seems to have spent its entire history waiting for Vesuvius to erupt, which goes some way towards explaining the local character traits of seize-the-day exuberance and a deep-seated reliance on superstitions to ward off harm. The superstitions that are part of everyday life are fascinating to outsiders: three times a year, the city holds its breath to see whether the Miracle of San Gennaro (*see p.xx*) will keep its citizens safe; the elaborate shrines dotted throughout the city are eloquent and touching testimonies to the faith of the populace; La Smorfia – an archaic dream dictionary – is widely used by locals to interpret their dreams and divine the winning lottery numbers; and the *corno* – a horn-shaped lucky charm supposed to ward off the evil eye – is possibly Naples' most popular souvenir.

with the revolutionary realism of his paintings. The works of his followers decorate churches and *palazzi* throughout the city.

CLIMATE

Spring and autumn are by far the best seasons for visiting the Bay of Naples. The weather from April to June and September to October is not too hot for sightseeing but still warm enough to swim. July and August can be unpleasantly hot and humid, especially in the city (hence the August exodus, when most shops and restaurants close). These two months are also peak season, when the islands and coastal resorts swarm with tourists. Winters are generally mild, though unless the ghostly, abandoned atmosphere of resorts off-season appeals, the coastal areas are less inviting. Bathing facilities close in early October and many restaurants and hotels close between November and Easter.

PEOPLE AND CUSTOMS

Like the rest of the Italian south, the pace of life here is unhurried and the easy-going locals place importance on the simple things in life – mainly good food and good company. The family is central to Neapolitan society, and many people live with their parents until well into their thirties. Compared with other major Italian cities,

Naples stubbornly refuses to make many concessions to tourism, so patience is essential: just trying to get across town can be something of an odyssey, thanks to its permanently clogged streets. The post-lunch siesta is commonly observed, and much of Naples shuts down on Sundays.

POLITICS AND ECONOMICS

Southern Italy suffers from high unemployment, poor infrastructure and a thriving black market. Moves are being made to address the problems of Italy's north–south divide and to combat corruption, but to little avail: the Camorra, the local branch of the mafia, has developed into one of Italy's most powerful organised-crime networks. The 2008 book and film *Gomorrah* by Roberto Saviano offered an alarming insight into the crisis, but in reality, the problem areas are on the outskirts and the tourist areas are as safe as in any other Italian city.

The biggest growth industry is tourism, although beyond Naples' grim industrial suburbs, swathes of vineyards, olive groves and citrus orchards ensure a reasonable income from agriculture, too.

Politically, Naples is neither strongly to the right nor to the left. Since World War II, both Christian Democrats and Democratic Socialists have governed the city with roughly equal frequency.

Above from far left: inside a *centro storico* church; Neapolitan graffiti; an appealing beverage.

Below: statuary of all kinds in Naples' *centro storico*.

FOOD AND DRINK

With an abundance of tasty, fresh produce, and a populace that takes its food very seriously indeed, you may well be tempted to give in to gluttony in Naples. Whether you're snacking on takeaway pizza or tucking into a seafood feast, expect to be left wanting more.

Above: be sure to visit a Naples gelateria.

Restaurant Hours
Restaurants generally open for business at around 12.30pm, but Neapolitans don't tend to eat until around an hour later; in the evening, restaurants open at around 7.30pm to cater to tourists, but the locals are generally still quaffing *aperitivi* at that hour, heading from bar to restaurant at about 9pm. Many restaurants in Naples are closed on Sunday.

The Italians' passion for food makes them demanding customers, which means that standards are universally high: you'll eat well even in the humblest of backstreet trattorias. Queues of locals are always a good sign – if they think the food's worth waiting for, then it invariably is. On Sundays and special occasions, a family day out involves an extended, multi-course lunch. The established seafront restaurants are inundated with hungry Neapolitans at weekends, so to avoid disappointment it's best to book.

LOCAL CUISINE

The defining characteristics of the local cuisine are freshness and simplicity: even in the more upscale places, no Neapolitan chef worthy of the name would consider sullying fish this fresh by drowning it in sauce. Thanks to the balmy climate and fertile volcanic terrain, the raw materials are of an exceptionally high quality, which is why pizza simply topped with ripe tomatoes, basil and local olive oil tastes better here than it does anywhere else on the planet. Aside from pizza, most menus in this coastal area revolve around fish (*pesce*), seafood (*frutti di mare*) and pasta.

Street Food
Naples is ideal for lunch on the run: *friggitorie* sell pizza by the slice, as well as delicious fried snacks that make a great picnic lunch. Try *arancini* (breaded rice balls stuffed with minced meat or mozzarella), *crocchè* (potato croquettes), *scagliuozze* (fried polenta) or *sciurilli* (fried courgette blossom).

Pizza
Naples is the birthplace of pizza. The authentic Neapolitan variety has a thin crust and is cooked quickly in a wood-fired oven. The classics are the *marinara* (oil, tomatoes, oregano and garlic) and the *margherita* (mozzarella, tomatoes and basil), Naples' bestseller. It was named after the Queen of Savoy, wife of the first Italian king, who appreciated its patriotic red, green and white topping. Other local favourites are the *capricciosa* (mozzarella, tomato, mushrooms, artichokes, olives and prosciutto) and *calzone* or *ripieno* (folded and stuffed with mozzarella, ricotta and salami).

Pasta

Pasta with seafood *(alla pescatora)* is a menu staple: *spaghetti alle vongole* (spaghetti with clams) and *zuppa di cozze* (mussel soup) are typical *primi*. *Spaghetti ai ricci di mare* (sea urchins) is a Procidan speciality. Non-fish pasta dishes include *pasta e fagioli* (pasta and beans), *pasta alla puttanesca* (tomatoes, olives, capers and chilli), and ravioli with ricotta and tomato sauce, Capri's speciality. *Scialatielli* is a popular pasta in Sorrento and along the Amalfi Coast, usually served with seafood, but sometimes with cannellini beans.

Fish and Seafood

Fish as a main course is simply prepared, but always fresh. Try it grilled *(alla griglia)*, fried *(fritto)* or cooked in a light broth *(all'acqua pazza)*. Squid and octopus *(polpo)* are Neapolitan favourites, usually stewed in a sauce of tomatoes, olive oil, peppers and garlic. *Fritto misto* is a popular dish of small fish from the bay, served fried, while *zuppa di pesce* (fish soup), more of a hearty stew than a soup, is eaten as a main course with toast.

Meat

Although fish is predominant, most menus offer at least a couple of meaty options. *Carne al ragù* is a typical dish made with rolls of meat cooked very slowly in a tomato sauce. *Coniglio all'ischitana* (rabbit stew) is an Ischian classic; Procida has its own version.

Sartù is an elaborate ring-shaped rice dish stuffed with a mixture of meats and vegetables.

Vegetables

The cornerstone of Campanian cooking is the *pomodoro* – the humble tomato. A little oil, onion, garlic, basil, parsley, maybe some capers and black olives to complement sun-ripened tomatoes, preferably the oblong San Marzano variety, known for their intense sweetness, go into making *salsa alla napoletana*. *Pomodorini* (cherry tomatoes) also make regular appearances in sauces and salads. *Parmigiana di melanzane*, an aubergine, tomato and mozzarella bake, is a delicious vegetarian option. Typical *contorni* (side dishes) include *scarola* and *friarelli* (local bitter greens) and *caponata*, similar to ratatouille, but with a generous dose of capers.

Above from far left: Naples is the birthplace of pizza; choosing from the many delights at Caffè Gambrinus *(see box, p.37)*.

Below: pasta with seafood is a winning combination.

PASTIERA NAPOLETANA 2.20€

Above from far left:
sweet *pastiera
napoletana* is eaten at
Easter; tomatoes and
mozzarella; *limoncello*
is a favourite tipple.

Cheeses

Campanian mozzarella is made from buffalo milk and has a distinctively milky taste and velvety texture. It is usually eaten as a starter with basil and tomato (*insalata caprese*), and is a key pizza ingredient. Mozzarella in *carrozza* ('in a carriage') is a thick slice of mozzarella fried between two slices of bread. Cow's-milk *scamorza* is delicious when smoked (*affu-* *micata*) and grilled. Fresh ricotta is widely used both in savoury dishes and cakes.

THE MENU

Lunch *(pranzo)* and dinner *(cena)* traditionally involve a starter *(antipasto)*, followed by a 'first course' *(primo)* of pasta, risotto or soup, and a 'second course' *(secondo)* of fish or meat accompanied by a side serving of vegetables *(contorni)*, ordered separately, rounded off with dessert *(dolce)*. That said, it is perfectly acceptable to share a plate of *antipasti*, then have a main course, say, or order simply a plate of pasta at lunch.

If you're having difficulty choosing, an *antipasto misto* (an assortment of starters) is a good way to sample local specialities. A typical mixed platter might include mozzarella, prosciutto and/or salami, fish or potato croquettes, *bruschetta* and grilled vegetables. And if you're really unsure of what to order and you're happy to experiment, ask the waiter to bring you *un piatto tipico* (a local dish).

WHERE TO EAT

The variety of venues dedicated to eating and drinking – from spit-and-sawdust pizzerias to gourmet fine-dining restaurants – is testimony to the important place that

Life is Sweet

There are *pasticcerie* everywhere you look in Naples, their shelves groaning with an abundance of pastries in every conceivable form: stuffed with cream, dusted with icing sugar, topped with dainty arrangements of glazed fruit, or slathered in the finest chocolate. Neapolitan classics include rum-soaked *babà* and fresh-from-the-oven *sfogliatelle*, fine-layered, shell-shaped pastry filled with orange-flavoured ricotta – as well as seasonal favourites such as *struffoli* (puffed-up balls of dough drenched in honey) at Christmas, and *zeppole di San Giuseppe* (deep-fried doughnuts stuffed with custard), baked to celebrate the saint's day on March 19. *Pastiera napoletana*, a ricotta cheesecake scented with orange blossom, has been baked to celebrate Easter for centuries.

BABA' LIMONE 2.20€ BABA'

16 OVERVIEW

food holds in Neapolitans' hearts. It is worth remembering that price and formality aren't necessarily an indicator of quality: that unprepossessing backstreet trattoria is likely to surprise you with a meal worthy of far fancier establishments.

Snacks

You are never more than five minutes from a café, pastry shop *(pasticceria)* or ice-cream parlour *(gelateria)*. Savoury snacks and cakes are usually eaten standing up or on the hoof. However, in summer there are plenty of pavement cafés with outdoor seating where you can nurse a drink, chat and people-watch for as long as you like.

Meals

Restaurant meals are eaten in either a ristorante or the traditionally simpler trattoria or osteria – though the distinction is somewhat blurred these days. Many restaurants serve pizza too, but pizzerias generally offer only pizza; a pizza *al taglio* is usually a hole-in-the-wall pizzeria selling slices to take away. A *tavola calda* is a cheap self-service place, offering hot and cold dishes.

DRINKS

The wines of the Italian south are enjoying a renaissance, and Campania produces some excellent varieties,

benefiting from an abundance of indigenous grapes and a favourable climate. The best of the local wines, such as Fiano and Falanghina, derive from ancient varieties introduced by the Greeks and Romans, and may well be the forebears of the more renowned Cabernet and Chardonnay. Greco di Tufo is a dry white, ideal with fish dishes or soups, while Falanghina and Fiano di Avellino are fruity yet dry. Ischia produces good local whites, notably Biancolella, cultivated on the steep slopes of Monte Epomeo.

Among the reds, the *aglianico* grape reigns supreme; Italy's longest-cultivated variety, it is thought to have been introduced to Campania by the Greeks in around 750BC. Nowadays, the grape goes into making the highly prized, full-bodied Taurasi.

Dinner is preceded by *aperitivi* – traditionally Prosecco – and followed by *digestivi* such as *grappa*, the Italian firewater. For those with a sweeter tooth there is *limoncello*, a strong but sweet lemon liqueur.

The morning coffee is usually knocked back at the counter rather than lingered over (and you'll be charged around double for the privilege of sitting down). Italians everywhere like to end a meal with a caffè, and the Neapolitan espresso is hailed as the best in the country, served very hot and very strong; if you like it weaker, ask for a macchiato (with a drop of hot milk).

Above: café culture.

Ice Cream
Ice cream *(gelato)* comes in a bewildering choice of flavours and is an essential accessory to the customary evening *passeggiata*. To ensure it's the real deal, check that it's *artigianale* (homemade). *Granita*, a crushed-ice drink usually flavoured with lemon, is wonderful on a hot day.

SHOPPING

Naples and the Amalfi Coast may not compete with Rome and Milan in terms of designer shopping, but a wealth of independent boutiques, traditional crafts and lively neighbourhood markets keep diehard shoppers amused.

Naples' main attraction for shoppers lies in the individuality of its boutiques and specialist shops, and the atmosphere of its shopping streets. To shop as the locals do, take it slowly, punctuating your window-shopping with plenty of breaks for *gelato* and coffee.

NAPLES

Whatever you buy, take home a local speciality to remind you of your trip: a bottle of *limoncello*, some spicy salami, a set of Christmas crib figurines or a pair of made-to-measure sandals.

Designer Fashion

Most of the up-market designer shops are in Chiaia. Via dei Mille and Via dei Filangeri, and their side streets, are crammed with boutiques selling clothes, shoes, leather goods, jewellery and soft furnishings. Big-name designers – Ferragamo, Armani, Versace, Gucci, et al – cluster around Piazza dei Martiri and Via Calabritto. Finely crafted bags, belts and leather goods can be found at Tramontano (Via Chiaia 143) while Marinella's legendary ties are worn by royalty and film stars (Riviera di Chiaia 287).

Mainstream Fashion

More affordable clothes and accessories can be found on Via Toledo at chains such as Benetton and Stefanel. The street is lined with pavement hawkers selling good imitations of designer handbags, scarves, watches, sunglasses and jewellery; haggling is expected. The Galleria Umberto I, an elegant 19th-century shopping arcade, is a retreat from the heat and crowds. Vomero is home to the department store Coin (Via Scarlatti 90–98), while Chiaia has the cheaper Upim (Via dei Mille 59).

Arts and Crafts

The *centro storico*, particularly along and around Spaccanapoli, is filled with artisans' workshops, jewellers, grocery stores and specialist shops: a great source of quirky souvenirs. You will often find an entire street dedicated to one particular product: Via San Sebastiano has back-to-back music shops; Via Santa Maria di Costantinopoli is good for antiques. A good place for a Neapolitan souvenir is Via di San Gregorio Armeno, full of stalls selling terracotta figures and kitsch paraphernalia for the decoration of Christmas cribs (*presepi*), alongside *smorfia* boards (a kind of dream-inter-

Opening Hours and Sales
Shops open 9.30am–1.30pm, then from 4pm until 7.30–8pm. Most are closed on Sundays, except for some *pasticcerie*, which open in the morning. Boutiques tend to be closed on Monday mornings in winter and Saturday afternoons in summer. Some food shops close on Thursday afternoons. Many shops shut in August, when Neapolitans take their holidays. The sales in Naples take place mid-January to mid-March and mid-July to mid-September.

preting lotto game) and horn-shaped good-luck charms – descendants of the phallic amulets of Pompeii.

Jewellery

The ancient art of engraving and cameo-making is still practised in Naples and in the factories of Torre del Greco on the outskirts. Spaccanapoli has several jewellers selling traditional designs, while the streets south of Corso Umberto and west of Via Duomo are the domain of gold- and silversmiths.

AMALFI COAST

The bright ceramics made around the Amalfi Coast, particularly Vietri sul Mare, are highly prized. Workshops *(botteghe)* are dotted along the coastal road, though it's not always easy to stop. Ravello and Amalfi have a good choice of shops selling quality ceramics.

The Amatruda family (www. amatruda.it) operates the last of Amalfi's paper mills, producing hand-made paper that is sold in beautifully packaged boxes all over town.

Positano is known for its clothes, swimwear and sandals *(see p.67)*.

SORRENTO

The main shopping street, Corso Italia, is dominated by fashion, footwear and jewellery stores; the more up-market boutiques are west of Piazza Tasso. The narrow pedestrian streets of Via San Cesareo and Via Fuoro are full of souvenir shops, selling lemon-themed teatowels, ceramics and soaps, as well as leather bags, lace and the ubiquitous *limoncello (see margin, p.61)*. Marquetry *(intarsio)* is Sorrento's other speciality. For quality pieces, visit A. Gargiulo & Jannuzzi (Viale E. Caruso 1).

CAPRI

The streets between the Piazzetta, Via Vittorio Emanuele and Via Camerelle are home to fashion's top names. The prices are prohibitive for most, but window-shopping is a time-honoured Capri pastime. For a cheaper souvenir, visit Carthusia (Viale Matteotti 2d), whose artisanal perfumes are made on-site; there are branches all over town and in Sorrento, Naples and Positano.

Above from far left: cameos are still popular in Naples; shopping on Via San Gregorio Armeno; kids' arts and crafts in Sorrento.

Naples' Markets

Naples' wealth of bustling street markets are great hunting grounds for foodie souvenirs – and offer an authentic slice of Neapolitan life in all its chaotic, colourful glory. Towards the station, the exuberant market around Porta Nolana is famous for its fish, but also sells fruit and vegetables. Via Pignasecca, the heart of working-class Naples, climbs from Piazza Carità (at the end of the pedestrianised section of Via Toledo) to Montesanto station. It's heaven for bargain-hunters and food-lovers, with its hotchpotch of fruit, fish and tripe stalls, bakeries and delis, and a great place to pick up local salamis and cheeses. The tiny food shops and stalls along Via dei Tribunali are good for *taralli* (Neapolitan savoury pastries), biscuits, pasta and local wines.

ENTERTAINMENT

Performance is part of Neapolitan life. The locals' innate flair for entertainment and penchant for theatrics are reflected in the city's cultural life, from world-class opera to classical concerts under the stars.

Naples is best known for its opera, but, as seems fitting for this earthy, down-to-earth city, it's the more populist, home-grown *canzone napoletana* (*see box, p.38*) that you're most likely to hear during your visit. Theatre in Naples is an Italian-only realm; the main venue is the Teatro Bellini (tel: 081-549 1266; www.teatrobellini.it).

Plenty of concerts and events are organised, particularly during the summer, but nightlife in these parts generally revolves around eating and drinking. The best way to enjoy the balmy nights is to join the locals for a postprandial stroll, with the essential ice-cream stop along the way.

MUSIC

Naples' prestigious Teatro San Carlo (*see p.36*) makes a suitably grand backdrop to the world-class performances that take place there, while on the coast and islands, a concert with a view is not to be missed.

Opera

The Teatro San Carlo is the oldest working opera house in Europe and Italy's best after Milan's La Scala. The season runs from January to mid-July, and from September to December. Buy tickets in the theatre box office or from the ticket office in Galleria Umberto I, opposite (tel: 081-551 9188; www.boxofficenapoli.it).

Classical Music

Outside Naples, classical-music lovers are well catered for all summer long. During the Sorrento Festival, concerts are held in the picturesque cloister of San Francesco church, while Ravello's prestigious music festival (*see box, p.72*), centred on the Villa Rufolo gardens, draws an international crowd. In Capri, open-air concerts are staged at the Certosa di San Giacomo and Villa San Michele. The neoclassical villas in and around Ercolano play host to the Festival delle Ville Vesuviane (tel: 081-732 2134; www.villevesuviane.net).

FILM

Virtually all English-language films are dubbed into Italian. Naples' film festival in June offers a rare opportunity to see films in their original language (www.napolifilmfestival.com).

Commedia Dell'arte
The *Commedia dell'arte*, in which stock characters play out a variety of plots on the eternal themes of love, jealousy, revenge and death, has ancient roots in Naples. Look out for Pulcinella – the female equivalent of Britain's Mr Punch – who crops up on any number of souvenirs, from puppets to key-rings, across the city. Actual performances these days are rare, but check www.guarattelle.it for details of forthcoming shows.

NIGHTLIFE

The liveliest places after dark are the main piazzas of the old town, especially around the university district, where the majority of late-night bars and live-music venues are clustered. Chiaia, too, has a lively after-dark scene, with chic cocktail lounges and some trendy clubs; be sure to dress up. Listings of what's on where can be found in the local newspaper, *Il Mattino*, or drop in at the tourist office for information and free entertainment guides.

During the summer, many city venues close and beach bars turn into clubs. The best place along the coast for all-night dancing is Positano.

FESTIVALS

Each city, town and village has its own patron saint, and their feast day *(festa)* is celebrated with parades and processions, elaborate costumes, singing and dancing, fireworks and feasting. Summer is the season for classical-music festivals, most of which begin in July. Autumn festivals, known as *sagre*, are linked to the land and harvest time.

Annual Events

The first major celebration of the year is Easter week, with large-scale Good Friday processions; Procida's is one of the most dramatic. In Naples,

the extraordinary thrice-yearly Festa di San Gennaro *(see margin, p.32)*, the first of which is in May, is not to be missed if you're in the city. Also in May, the Maggio dei Monumenti allows access to historic buildings normally closed to the public (ask at the tourist office for a programme).

From July to September, open-air concerts take place in the spectacular Villa Rufolo in Ravello. July is a bumper month for saints' days: on the 16th, the bell tower of the church of the Madonna del Carmine on Naples' Piazza del Mercato explodes with fireworks; on the 26th, the patron saint of Ischia, Sant'Anna, is honoured with a torchlit procession of hundreds of boats; the 27th is the Festa di San Pantaleone, with the liquefaction of the saint's blood and a spectacular fireworks display in Ravello.

August 15 is Ferragosto (the feast of the Assumption) and a national holiday. Positano has a procession to commemorate the landing of the Saracens, followed by yet more pyrotechnics. September sees the Piedigrotta Festival, a traditional celebration of Neapolitan songs, as well as Pizzafest, a 10-day celebration of the doughy disc.

Finally, Christmas *(Natale)* in Naples is a colourful affair: churches compete to build the finest *presepe* (Nativity scene, *see box, p.34*), and concerts are held around the city.

Above from far left: Naples' film festival is held every June; a performance at Teatro San Carlo; cracking open the Prosecco.

Above: the Teatro San Carlo.

SPORTS AND OUTDOOR ACTIVITIES

This famed stretch of coast offers opportunities galore for outdoor types: hire a boat, take a diving course or stick to dry land and tackle one of the hiking trails that crisscross the countryside.

Above: the Amalfi Coast is ideal for boat trips.

Naples' open spaces are perfect for running and cycling, but for swimming and watersports you're better off on the coast. For Ischia's famous spas, see the box on p.80. A full list of sports facilities in Naples, from bowling alleys to tennis courts, can be found on the tourist office's website, www.inaples.it.

SWIMMING

Most of the coastline from Naples to Salerno is rocky, as it is on the islands, and beaches are not always accessible or easy to find. In the Naples area, the cleanest water is at Posillipo, west of town, although the beaches are overrun in high season. On the Sorrentine Peninsula, the Bay of Ieranto *(see p.65)* is many people's idea of a perfect, hidden-away beach; Sorrento itself is less blessed, though there are plenty of *stabilimenti* (beach clubs) where you can lounge around in the sun. Some of the fancier hotels in Sorrento and Amalfi have lifts down to the sea and their own sea-water pools and private beaches.

The Amalfi Coast's grey-sand beaches are not the most picturesque, but Positano's and Amalfi's are broad at least, and the sea is clear enough. Capri's shore, although pebbly, offers plenty of opportunities for a dip; Marina Grande is the most accessible, but the section by the Blue Grotto is more appealing, with platforms carved out of the rock and ladders down to the sea. Ischia has some lovely sandy beaches; the Baia di San Montano and the Spiaggia dei Maronti are the ones to head for. On Procida, the Lido and Chiaia are the nicest beaches.

Super-fit swimmers compete in the Gulf Marathon (www.caprinapoli. com) every year in June, an epic 36km (22-mile) slog from Capri's Marina Grande to Naples' seafront.

DIVING

The Gulf of Naples offers plenty of opportunities for experienced divers and beginners alike, and there are a number of dive centres offering diving trips from around €70, courses and equipment. On the mainland, try

Centro Sub Costiera Amalfitana (Via Marina di Praia, Praiano, tel: 089-812 148; www.centrosub.it). On Ischia, contact Ischia Diving Centre (Via Iasolino 106, Ischia Porto, tel: 081-981 852). Procida's limpid blue waters are perfect for diving. Procida Diving Centre (tel: 081-896 8385 or 338-722 7484; www. vacanzeaprocida.it) organise dives with an instructor and equipment.

Diving in the Campi Flegrei is a particularly rewarding excursion (contact Centro Sub Campi Flegrei, tel: 081-853 1563; www.centrosubcampiflegrei. it), and the crystal-clear waters of the protected Marine Park of Punta della Campanella on the Sorrentine Peninsula is another popular spot. Futuro Mare (tel: 081-877 1472; www.sorrentodiving.it) organises daily excursions, including trips to the Marine Park and around Capri, Ischia and Procida.

BOATING

You can hire boats all along the coast. In Procida, try Blue Dream (tel: 081-896 0579; www.bluedreamcharter.com), which rents yachts and runs a sailing school. If a yacht is beyond your budget, try Ippocampo (tel: 081-658 7667; www.ippocampo.biz), which rents dinghies and the local *gozzi* boats, as well as organising diving excursions, both day and night. In Ischia, Capitan Morgan (tel: 081-985 080; www.capitanmorgan. it) runs inexpensive boat trips round the island and to other points on the coast.

In Capri, Gruppo Motoscafisti operates boat trips round the island, while Capritime (tel: 329-214 9811; www. capritime.com) offers small-group boat tours with a skipper. For boat trips from Positano around the Amalfi Coast, see the box on p.68.

WALKING

The Sorrentine peninsula, the Monti Lattari and Amalfi Coast, Ischia and Capri all offer scenic walking trails, many marked out by the Club Alpino Italiano (CAI). The maps of the Sorrentine Peninsula and Ischia and Procida published by Kompass are useful for hikers. Footpaths have also been marked out on the slopes of Mount Vesuvius and Monte Faito *(see margin, p.58)*. Local tourist offices supply free walking maps. For organised excursions, contact Giovanni Visetti (tel: 339-694 2911), a friendly and knowledgeable local guide; his website, www.giovis. com, is an excellent resource.

RUNNING

The annual Naples Marathon (www. napolimarathon.it) is held mid-April, taking in the city centre and the Lungomare; there's also a half-marathon and a 4km (2½-mile) fun run. If you just want a leisurely jog, the broad, sweeping Lungomare is perfect; alternatively, head for the unpolluted air of the Bosco di Capodimonte.

Above from far left: swimming near Sorrento; Ischia is a walker's paradise.

Amusement Parks
Edenlandia (Viale Kennedy 76, Fuorigrotta; tel: 081-239 4090; www. edenlandia.it) is a traditional theme park just outside Naples, complete with rollercoaster, dodgems, merry-go-rounds and Disney characters; take the Cumana train from Montesanto to get there. The Città della Scienza (Via Coroglio 104; tel: 081-7352 600; www. cittadellascienza.it) is part of the redevelopment programme of the old Bagnoli steelworks. The hi-tech hands-on science park is a fun day out for children and adults; take bus R7 from Naples' Piazza Vittoria.

HISTORY: KEY DATES

Naples' fascinating, multi-layered history is tightly woven into the city's fabric: the layout of the 'centro storico' follows the grid of ancient Neapolis beneath it, while waves of invaders, including the French and the Spanish, constructed churches and palazzi in distinctive architectural styles.

GREEKS AND ROMANS

Naples '44
For an insight into how Naples' recent history has shaped the city, read Norman Lewis's fascinating *Naples '44*: a no-holds-barred memoir of the Allied occupation during World War II, when the city was stripped to its bare bones. The day-to-day dealings of the people are told as a series of humorous, tragic and astonishing anecdotes that help to shed light on some of the more eccentric characteristics of its present-day citizens.

*c.*700BC	Greeks establish a colony at Parthenope.
474BC	Greeks defeat the Etruscans and establish the new city of Neapolis near Parthenope. The two cities eventually merge to form one.
*c.*400BC	Neapolis is commercial capital of Campania, northernmost province of Magna Graecia.
326BC	Rome conquers Neapolis.
26BC	Tiberius retires to Capri, from where he rules the Roman Empire.
AD79	Vesuvius erupts, destroying Pompeii and Herculaneum.
324	Constantine becomes the first Christian Roman Emperor, ruling the Empire from Constantinople.

GOTHS, LOMBARDS AND NORMANS

410	Rome sacked by the Goths.
536	Naples falls to the Eastern empire.
568	The Lombards start to overrun Italy and the south is divided between Byzantine and Lombard rulers.
1139	Naples falls to the Normans.
1194	Henry VI of Germany conquers the Norman kingdom of Sicily and becomes King of Naples.
1197–1250	Frederick, Henry's son, achieves absolute rule over the city, bringing good government and founding Naples' first university.

THE ANGEVINS AND ARAGONESE

1266	Kingdom of Naples given to the French royal house of Anjou.
1268	Charles makes Naples his royal residence.
1309–43	Robert of Anjou becomes king of Naples and brings Giotto and Petrarch to the court.

1442	King Alfonso of Aragon conquers the Kingdom of Naples and unites it with the Kingdom of Sicily, also under Aragon rule. His court becomes the centre of southern Italian humanism.	Above from far left: a victim of the AD79 eruption of Mount Vesuvius; French King Louis XVIII meeting Caroline, Princess of Naples, in 1816.
1503	Naples is ruled by Spanish viceroys for the next two centuries.	
1529	Plague rages in the city. Over 60,000 people perish.	
1532	Viceroy Don Pedro of Toledo carries out urban development.	
1647	Poverty and oppression provoke a massive people's revolt led by a Neapolitan fisherman, Masaniello. The revolt is violently quashed.	
1656	Plague returns, claiming over 250,000 of Naples' inhabitants.	
1707	The Austrian Habsburgs gain control of most of Spain's Italian territories, including Naples.	

THE BOURBONS

1738	Austria loses power over the Kingdoms of Naples and Sicily to the Spanish Bourbons.
1806	Napoleon's brother, Joseph Bonaparte, takes control of Naples.
1815	Bourbons return to the throne after Napoleon's defeat at Waterloo.
1860	Garibaldi defeats the Bourbons and enters Naples, making it part of a newly unified Kingdom of Italy.
1880–1914	More than 2.5 million Italians emigrate to the Americas.
1884	Severe cholera epidemic.

WORLD WAR II TO THE PRESENT DAY

1943	Naples is bombed by Allied forces. After a four-day uprising by the people, the German occupying troops are driven from the city.	
1980	Campania struck by earthquake; 3,000 killed with thousands left homeless.	
1994	Following the *Mani Pulite* (clean hands) anti-corruption campaign, Antonio Bassolino is elected mayor of Naples and begins a massive clean-up campaign.	**Below:** a Mafia trial in Naples.
2002	The lira is replaced by the euro.	
2008	A severe rubbish crisis sees piles of refuse left uncollected in Naples' streets. The crisis is linked to the mafia, who run a lucrative business out of waste disposal.	
2010	Prime Minister Silvio Berlusconi holds crisis talks in Naples to resolve ongoing mafia-related crime.	

WALKS AND TOURS

THE CENTRO STORICO

The atmospheric alleys of Naples' historic centre harbour many of the city's most intriguing sights, and give a real flavour of its exhilarating street life. Wander the ancient streets and feast your eyes: this is Naples at its heady, high-octane best.

DISTANCE 3.5km (2¼ miles)
TIME A full day
START Piazza del Gesù Nuovo
END Piazza Bellini
POINTS TO NOTE
You won't be able to visit all the churches mentioned in one day, especially as many close around noon, either for the rest of the day or until around 4pm. One option is to split the itinerary into two, allocating one morning to Spaccanapoli and another to Via dei Tribunali. If you're short of time, the must-sees are Santa Chiara, the Sansevero chapel, the Duomo and San Lorenzo Maggiore. The area is at its liveliest in the evening, so be sure to come back for dinner in one of the area's many pizzerias – a quintessential Naples experience.

Naples' *Guglie*
Keep an eye out for the soaring *guglie* (marble spires) that embellish three of the old town's squares. The first, dedicated to the Virgin, stands outside the Gesù Nuovo church; the second, on Piazza San Domenico, gave thanks for the end of the plague epidemic; the third, in Piazza Sisto Riario Sforza, was erected in honour of San Gennaro, Naples' patron saint, when the city escaped unscathed after Vesuvius erupted in 1631.

Naples' *centro storico* is a dense network of shadowy, narrow alleys and small squares built on the site of ancient Neapolis. Fanning upwards from the harbour and bordered by Via Toledo to the west and Piazza Garibaldi to the east, the old town is crammed with everything from cavernous churches and grand *palazzi*, to cramped houses, shops and cafés.

The most important sights are concentrated along two parallel east-west thoroughfares that formed part of the ancient street grid: Spaccanapoli and Via dei Tribunali. This is now one of Naples' most compelling quarters, and a wander through the district yields no end of photo opportunities: fishmongers hawk their produce at top volume, baskets are lowered from top-floor windows to be loaded with purchases from shops below, and mopeds zip through the human traffic, klaxons blaring.

SPACCANAPOLI

Spaccanapoli (literally, 'split Naples') is the series of narrow streets that run in a long, straight line from Via Toledo to the Greek walls.

Chiesa del Gesù Nuovo

The walk starts at Piazza del Gesù Nuovo, a bustling square dominated by the grey ashlar facade of the **Chiesa**

del Gesù Nuovo ❶ (tel: 081-557 8111; Mon–Sat 7am–12.30pm, 4–7pm; Sun 7am–2pm, 4–7pm; free), originally part of a Renaissance *palazzo* that was converted into a church by Jesuits in 1597. The Baroque interior is filled with fine frescoes, paintings and sculptures, including works by the Spanish artist José Ribera (1590–1652) and the master of Neapolitan Baroque Luca Giordano (1632–1705).

Santa Chiara

The first of Spaccanapoli's streets is Via Benedetto Croce. Immediately on the right stands the **convent of Santa Chiara ❷** (tel: 081-552 1597; www. santachiara.info; church: Mon–Sat 7.30am–1pm, 4.40–8pm, free; cloister and museum: Mon–Sat 9.30am–5.30pm, Sun 9.30am–2.30pm; charge). Although bomb damage during World War II destroyed much of the interior, reconstruction has

Above from far left: Via dei Tribunali; tiles at the convent of Santa Chiara.

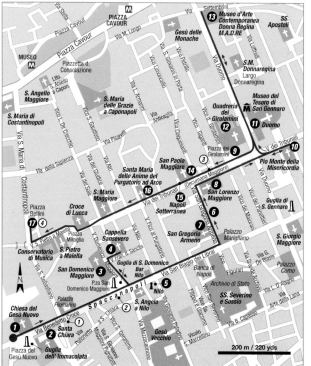

Above: inside Santa Chiara convent.

Forbidden Seat
Santa Chiara's pretty majolica-tiled benches may look like the perfect place to take the weight off, but vigilant guards employed to protect the precious tiles will tell you off if you try to take a seat.

Above from left:
the atmospheric
interior of San
Domenico Maggiore;
courtyard at San
Gregorio Armeno; San
Lorenzo Maggiore.

Weird Science
Even as an old
man, Raimondo di
Sangro's mind was
impressively agile.
In July 1770, he
made his last public
appearance, crossing
the waters of the bay
on an ornate 'sea-
going carriage' that
he had designed
himself, which
ploughed through the
waves thanks to an
ingenious system of
paddle wheels. A few
months later, his most
extreme experiment –
to test a supposed
elixir of life – caused
his death.

preserved the austere character of the original church, built in the early 14th century for Robert of Anjou. His tomb lies behind the main altar. Fragments of a fresco by Giotto can be seen in the convent choir. The serene cloister, decorated with majolica tiles and planted with citrus trees, is one of the most photographed corners of Naples. A small museum displays a selection of liturgical objects salvaged from the bomb wreckage, but most interesting is the excavated area that reveals parts of an old Roman bath complex (1st century AD).

A few paces further on the right is **Gay Odin**, see ⑪①, a good excuse to stop for an ice cream.

San Domenico Maggiore

Next stop is Piazza San Domenico Maggiore, flanked by 16th- to 17th-century *palazzi* and the Gothic church of **San Domenico Maggiore** ❸ (tel: 081-557 3204; daily 9.30am–noon, 5–7pm; free). One of several churches commissioned by Charles I of Anjou, it was given a Baroque makeover in the 17th century, then remodelled in the 19th century in an attempt to restore something of its Gothic grandeur. The upper gallery of the sacristy is lined with the tombs of kings and nobles of the Aragonese court. The inlaid marble altar and balustrade is by Cosimo Fanzago (1591–1678), leading sculptor and architect of his day.

Cappella Sansevero

Take a left turn up Via Domenico Maggiore, then right on to Via Francesco de Sanctis for one of Naples' unmissable sights, the **Cappella Sansevero** ❹ (tel: 081-551 8470; www.museosansevero. it; Mon and Wed–Sat 10am–6pm, Sun 10am–1.30pm; charge). The burial chapel of the noble di Sangro family is crammed with sculptural monuments commissioned by the eccentric Raimondo di Sangro, seventh prince of Sansevero (1710–71). The prince, a gifted scientist and inventor, was obsessed with alchemy *(see margin, left)* – the two cadavers in the crypt are supposedly the product of one of his wild experiments. In the centre of the nave is the incredibly lifelike *Cristo Velato* (Veiled Christ) by Giuseppe Sammartino, sculpted in 1753. The rendering in alabaster of the soft folds and the translucence of the veil draped over Christ's prostrate body is remarkable.

Back on the square, stop for a coffee at the historic **Scaturchio**, see ⑪②, whose outside tables are perfectly placed for taking in the melee of students from the nearby university, scooter-dodging tourists and chattering locals.

Via di San Gregorio Armeno

Proceed along Spaccanapoli (you are now on Via San Biagio dei Librai), past the **statue of the Nile** ❺ on your left. The reclining figure is the Egyptian river god; the cherubs symbolise the river's tributaries. Peek into the tiny

Bar Nilo opposite to pay your respects at the shrine to another much-revered figure, the Argentine footballer Diego Maradona. A little further along, turn left into **Via San Gregorio Armeno** ❻. This narrow side street is entirely dedicated to the Neapolitan obsession with *presepi* – Christmas cribs *(see box, p.34)*. Stalls piled high with carved crib figurines, hand-crafted backdrops complete with ruins, trees and water features, fairy lights and baubles, lotto game boards and priapic good-luck charms spill out on to the street. Amongst the shepherds and wise men, look out for the modern-day heroes and villains, Barack Obama, Silvio Berlusconi and David Beckham among them.

If you reach the **church and convent of San Gregorio Armeno** ❼ (Via di San Gregorio Armeno 1; tel: 081-552 0186; daily 9am–noon, Sun until 1pm; free) before it closes, pop in to admire the interior, which is a riot of Baroque ornamentation, featuring frescoes by Luca Giordano.

San Lorenzo Maggiore

At the top of the street is the church of **San Lorenzo Maggiore** ❽ (tel: 081-211 0860; www.san lorenzomaggiorenapoli.it; Mon–Sat 8am–12.30pm, 5.30–7pm, Sun 8am–12.30pm; free), another Angevin commission. Parts of the church, including the facade, were rebuilt in the 18th century, but most of the interior has been restored to its Gothic

original. Skirting the altar is a magnificent semicircular ribbed vault. Sections of glass in the transept floor reveal the remains of a Roman mosaic.

To see more of the Greco-Roman city that lies beneath, buy a ticket to the **archaeological site** (Mon–Fri 9.30am–5pm, Sat 9.30am–7pm, Sun 9.30am–1pm; charge). A flight of steps takes you down to a section of the old Greco-Roman road that has been excavated here. It led to the forum or *agora*, still buried in the foundations of San Paolo church. Works are ongoing, but so far they have exposed the city treasure house *(aerarium)*, a dyer's *(fullonica)*, a laundry *(lavanderia)* and parts of a Roman market *(macellum)*.

Cappella del Monte di Pietà

If you're visiting at the weekend, find time to visit the lovely Cappella del Monte di Pietà, with a 17th-century frescoed ceiling and statues by Pietro Bernini on its facade. It's hidden away inside the Banca di Napoli at Via San Biagio dei Librai 114, and only open on Saturdays (9am–7pm), Sundays and holidays (9am–2pm). Entrance is free.

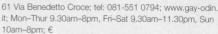

Food and Drink

① GAY ODIN

61 Via Benedetto Croce; tel: 081-551 0794; www.gay-odin. it; Mon–Thur 9.30am–8pm, Fri–Sat 9.30am–11.30pm, Sun 10am–8pm; €

This historic chocolatier and *gelateria* has been keeping sweet-toothed Neapolitans happy for over a century. Now with branches all over the city, it's a wonderful place to shop for edible souvenirs – the chocolates are delicious and beautifully wrapped – and the gourmet ice creams are just as tempting. The chocolate flavours are the ones to go for, of course: try the cocoa bean, or the chocolate and ginger.

② SCATURCHIO

19 Piazza San Domenico Maggiore; tel: 081-551 6944; daily 7.20am–8.40pm; €

This long-established café not only serves an excellent cappuccino but is a great place to sample the classic Neapolitan sweets – *babà*, *sfogliatelle* and *pastiera*. The *ministeriali* – delectable coin-shaped chocolates stamped with the name of the bar's founder, Giovanni Scaturchio – look almost too good to eat.

VIA DEI TRIBUNALI

You are now on **Via dei Tribunali** (also known as the Decumano Maggiore), which arrows from Piazza Bellini to the Castel Capuano, and is as lively as Spaccanapoli, with the same dawn-to-dusk exuberance. Its abundance of excellent pizzerias makes Via dei Tribunali a good place to break for lunch; **Di Matteo**, see ⑪③, is one of the best.

Above: *centro storico* scenes.

Piazza dei Girolamini

Continuing east to **Piazza dei Girolamini ❾**, you'll come across some examples of the age-old local *rigattiere* (bric-a-brac) trade, with shops selling all manner of junk (or treasure, depending on your point of view), from Communion goblets to broken accordions and fragments of antique statuary – a good place to hunt for quirky souvenirs.

The Miracle of San Gennaro

Three times a year (the Saturday before the first Sunday in May, 19 September, and 16 December), devotees flock to the Duomo to witness the liquefying of San Gennaro's dried blood. If the 'miracle' fails to occur, the superstitious say disaster will strike.

Food and Drink 🍽

③ DI MATTEO

94 Via dei Tribunali; tel: 081-455 262; www.pizzeriadimatteo.it; Mon–Sat 10am–midnight; €
Whether or not its claim to have invented the pizza margherita (on 4 April 1936, apparently) is to be believed, Di Matteo is the archetypal Neapolitan pizzeria: rowdy, chaotic and very, very cheap. Head upstairs to soak up the atmosphere and (appetite permitting) go for the house speciality, *ripieno fritto* (fried calzone).

Pio Monte della Misericordia

Cross busy Via Duomo and continue on Via dei Tribunali for the small church and picture gallery of **Pio Monte della Misericordia ❿** (tel: 081-446 944; www.piomontedella misericordia.it; church: Mon–Tue, Thur–Fri 10.30am–2pm, Sat–Sun 9am–2.30pm, free; art gallery: Thur–Tue 9am–2.30pm, charge), famous for Caravaggio's immense altarpiece, the *Seven Acts of Mercy* (1607). The upstairs picture gallery displays works by some of the leading lights of Neapolitan Baroque: Luca Giordano, Massimo Stanzione and Giuseppe Ribera.

The Duomo

Back on Via Duomo, walk uphill to reach the **Duomo ⓫** (tel: 081-449 097; www.duomodinapoli.it; church: daily 9am–1.30pm, 2.30–7pm, free; museum: Tue–Sat 9.30am–2pm, charge; archaeological area and baptistry: Mon–Sat 9am–1pm, 4.30–7pm, Sun 9am–1pm, charge), whose ungainly neo-Gothic facade conceals a fine medieval building. The main attraction of the Baroque interior, in the **Cappella di San Gennaro**, is a precious silver bust containing phials of the blood of the city's patron saint *(see margin, left)*. The chapel glitters with more silver busts of saints, an exquisite silver altar in relief and a gilded bronze gate by Cosimo Fanzago. Access to the baptistry (550AD) and the Greek and

Roman remains of previous buildings on the site (closed for restoration at the time of writing) is from the left-hand nave. The next-door **Museo del Tesoro di San Gennaro** features paintings, silverware and ex-votos dedicated to the saint.

Opposite the Duomo, and reached through a lovely cloister planted with lemon trees, the small **Quadreria dei Girolamini** ⑫ (Via Duomo 142; tel: 081-294 444; Mon–Sat 9.30am–12.30pm; free) has fine paintings from the 16th–18th centuries.

M.A.D.RE

Further up Via Duomo, turn right on to Via Settembrini for Naples' key collection of modern art: the Museo d'Arte Contemporanea Donna Regina, or **M.A.D.RE** ⑬ (tel: 081-292 833; www.museomadre.it; Mon, Wed–Fri 10am–9pm, Sat–Sun 10am–midnight; charge, free Mon). On the first floor are site-specific works by artists such as Anish Kapoor and Jeff Koons; look out also for Jannis Kounellis' gigantic anchor and Rebecca Horn's unsettling *Spiriti*, with swivelling mirrors concealing ranks of skulls, set to eerie music.

On the second floor is an impressive collection of works by contemporary greats on long-term loan – Andy Warhol, Jasper Johns and Damien Hirst among them. The complex also includes the beautifully restored 14th-century church of Santa Maria Donnaregina Vecchia, now used for temporary exhibitions.

San Paolo Maggiore

Backtrack to Via dei Tribunali. About halfway along is the imposing church of **San Paolo Maggiore** ⑭ (tel: 081-454 048; church: Mon–Sat 9am–6pm, Sun 10am–12.30pm; crypt: Mon–Sat 8.30am–noon, 5–7.30pm, Sun 8.30am–6pm; free), built in the 16th century on the site of a temple to Castor and Pollux.

Napoli Sotterranea

Next door is the entrance to **Napoli Sotterranea** ⑮ (tel: 081-296 944; www.napolisotterranea.org; guided tours only Mon–Fri at noon, 2pm and 4pm, with additional tour Thur at 9pm; Sat–Sun at 10am, noon, 2pm, 4pm and 6pm; duration of tour 90mins; charge), a fascinating journey through underground Naples. Steps lead 40m (131ft) underground to the tunnels and chambers of the vast Greco-Roman aqueduct that supplied the city with its water until the cholera epidemic of 1884. Sections of the disused aqueduct were used as shelters during the heavy Allied bombardments of World War II. Claustrophobics beware – to reach one chamber you have to squeeze through some very narrow tunnels, lighting your way with a candle – but there's no better place to get a feel for the city's multi-layered history.

Above from far left: flags and flowers on Via dei Tribunali; Duomo paintings; detail of the facade of the Duomo.

Rooftop Art
It's not signposted, but you can ask the staff at M.A.D.RE to show you to the roof terrace, where a single sculpture – Mimmo Paladino's *Cavallo* ('Horse') – lords it over the city below.

Above from left: leafy Piazza Bellini; the Castel Nuovo's imposing towers flank the Renaissance Triumphal Arch.

Santa Maria delle Anime del Purgatorio ad Arco

On the last stretch of Via dei Tribunali, the bronze skulls on the railings outside the 17th-century church of **Santa Maria delle Anime del Purgatorio ad Arco** (tel: 081-551 0547; Mon–Sat 10am–1pm; charge for hypogeum) indicate that this is no ordinary church. It was long used for the worship of the dead, a practice officially forbidden by the Vatican, and the hypogeum still contains a pile of venerated bones.

Piazza Bellini

At Piazza Miraglia, Via dei Tribunali becomes Via San Pietro a Maiella, and passes the Gothic church of San Pietro a Maiella and the **Conservatorio di Musica** (tel: 081-564 4411), with a lovely courtyard where the strains of students practising their instruments sounds like an orchestra tuning up; ask at the desk about performances in the recital hall. Turn right into leafy **Piazza Bellini** ⓱ and peer down at the section of Greco-Roman wall in the middle, before settling down to a well-deserved *aperitivo* on the shady terrace of **Intra Moenia**, see ⓽④.

Food and Drink

④ **INTRA MOENIA**

70 Piazza Bellini; tel: 081-290 720; www.intramoenia.it; daily 10am–2pm; €

With its prime position on pretty Piazza Bellini, this café-bookshop is a popular spot throughout the day for drinks, snacks and light meals such as omelettes, sandwiches and salads, but it comes into its own at *aperitivo* hour, when the tables on the plant-filled terrace are in high demand.

Neapolitan *Presepi*

No Neapolitan household would be complete without its *presepe* (crib) at Christmas, but in Naples, the Nativity scene is as crowded as the city streets, with an exuberant cast of extras – children, musicians, peasants, farmers, dogs and chickens – rubbing shoulders with the usual shepherds, kings and angels. Figurine carving is still considered an art form and even if you're not in Naples at Christmas time, you'll find plenty of opportunities to admire it. The artisans in Via Gregorio Armeno do a roaring trade *(see p.31)*, and many of the larger churches display *presepi* year-round, each with their own cast of Neapolitan characters, usually depicted with unforgiving realism, in contrast to the delicate execution of the saints and angels. Don't miss the wonderful examples in Santa Chiara *(see p.29)* and the San Martino monastery *(see p.42)*.

ROYAL NAPLES

A full-day tour revealing Naples' monumental side. Marvel at the residences that were the hub of the Italian monarchy for over a thousand years, before joining the locals in a traditional seafront stroll.

The port of Naples is the maritime gateway to the city, an always-heaving transport hub that is key to the city's infrastructure. Ferries and hydrofoils that shuttle commuters and day-trippers up and down the coast and across to the islands jostle for space with gigantic cruise and container ships. Standing guard over the port on traffic-choked Piazza Municipio is the unmistakeable bulk of the Castel Nuovo (also known as the Maschio Angioino), the starting point of this tour of Royal Naples.

> **DISTANCE** 5km (3 miles)
> **TIME** A full day
> **START** Castel Nuovo
> **END** Via Chiaia
> **POINTS TO NOTE**
> The R2, R3, C4 and C82 buses all stop at Piazza Municipio. If possible, take this tour on a Sunday – the traditional day for a seafront stroll – to join the Neapolitans out for their weekly constitutional.

CASTEL NUOVO

The **Castel Nuovo** ❶ (tel: 081-795 5877; Mon–Sat 9am–7.30pm, last entrance 6pm, Sun 9am–1.30pm; charge) was called the 'new castle' to distinguish it from its predecessors, the Castel Capuano and Castel dell'Ovo. Built for Charles I of Anjou in 1279, the Angevin castle became a centre of culture, attracting a host of illustrious writers and artists, including Giotto, whose frescoes in the chapel and main hall are barely visible today. The Angevins were ousted by the Aragonese in 1443, and the castle was reconstructed under Alfonso I.

The Interior

Sandwiched between two of the five cylindrical towers, the gleaming Renaissance **Triumphal Arch** is a testament to the cultural renewal of Naples by the House of Aragon. The doors depict the victory of Aragonese over Angevins; these are replicas of the original doors, which can be seen inside the museum, complete with embedded cannonball. The central relief panel above the entrance arch shows Alfonso's triumphant entry into the city.

Across the courtyard, the **Palatine Chapel** is all that remains of the original 13th-century structure, and

Crocodile Fears
According to legend, a crocodile was shipped in from Egypt to devour errant prisoners in the Castel Nuovo's dungeon.

Above: the grand interior of the Palazzo Reale.

Budget Opera
Last-minute tickets to world-class performances at the Teatro San Carlo are available to under-30s for just €15, an hour before curtain-up.

is now part of the **Museo Civico**, which displays mainly Neapolitan paintings, sculptures and bronzes from the 18th–20th centuries over three floors. Don't miss the stately **Hall of the Barons**, with its spectacular rib-vaulted ceiling that soars to a height of 28m (92ft). Named after a group of rebellious noblemen executed here by King Ferdinand I for plotting his murder, it is now more prosaically used for city council meetings.

TEATRO SAN CARLO

Turn left out of Castel Nuovo and walk along Via Vittorio Emanuele to Via San Carlo and Piazza Trieste e Trento. Just before the square on your left is the **Teatro San Carlo ❷** (tel: 081-553 4565; www.teatrosancarlo.it; tours Mon–Sat 10am–5.30pm, 40 mins; charge), Italy's largest and oldest opera house, predating the Scala in Milan by 40 years. Commissioned by Charles of Bourbon in 1737 and completed in just

eight months, it quickly became one of the most important social venues in 18th-century Naples – and the stage of many a scandalous liaison. The plush six-tiered auditorium, all red velvet and gold stucco, can seat up to 3,000. Tickets generally cost from €50 to upwards of €100, but watching a performance here is a rare treat.

VIA TOLEDO AND THE QUARTIERI SPAGNOLI

On the opposite side of Via San Carlo, underneath the arcade, is the main entrance to the **Galleria Umberto I** ❸. The magnificent glass-roofed gallery, built in 1890, is lined with smart shops and cafés; the western exit brings you out on to **Via Toledo** ❹, Naples' main shopping street *(see p.18)*.

The grid of streets leading west off Via Toledo make up the **Quartieri Spagnoli** ❺ (Spanish Quarter). Originally built to house the Spanish military, the cramped dwellings became home to Naples' working classes. Take a detour (keeping your wits about you) into the labyrinth of narrow streets festooned with lines of washing that have become an evocative symbol of inner-city Naples.

PIAZZA PLEBISCITO

You will certainly have spotted the traffic-free expanse of the Piazza Plebiscito by now. Before heading over there, stop for a coffee at **Caffè Gambrinus**, see ❶❶. In 1994, **Piazza Plebiscito** – the 'People's Square' – was reclaimed by the people. Until then, this magnificent square had been used as a car park, but was cleared of traffic as part of a citywide clean-up in the 1990s. The semicircular piazza is embraced by the twin arcades of **San Francesco di Paola** (tel: 081-764 5133; daily 8am–noon, 3.30–7pm, Sun 8am–1pm; free), an imposing neoclassical church inspired by the Pantheon in Rome. The two equestrian statues gracing the square commemorate the two Bourbon kings, Ferdinand I and Charles III; both are by Canova.

The Palazzo Reale

Opposite the church, the **Palazzo Reale** ❻ (Piazza Plebiscito 1; tel: 081-400 547; www.palazzoreale napoli.it; Thur–Tue 9am–8pm, ticket office closes 7pm; charge) is the highlight of this tour. Built in the middle

Above: statuary in the Palazzo Reale.

Food and Drink 🍴

① CAFFÈ GAMBRINUS

Via Chiaia 1–2; tel: 081-417 582; Sun–Thur 7am–1am, Fri 7am–2am, Sat 7am–3am; €

This elegant Art Nouveau café, decked out with marble and chandeliers, dates from 1860. Once a popular haunt of artists, writers and politicians, it's now a time-honoured favourite for coffee and pastries during the day, early-evening *aperitivi* and pre-clubbing pick-me-ups.

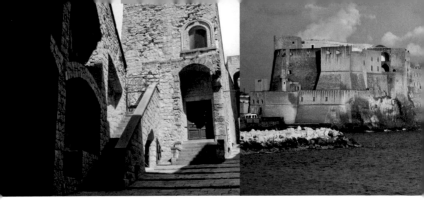

Magic Egg
According to legend, buried in the rock beneath the Castel dell'Ovo lies an ancient egg *(uovo)*, which holds the fate of the city within its shell. The Roman poet Virgil, believed to possess powers of divination, prophesied that if the egg broke, catastrophe would befall the city.

of the 16th century, its design was tweaked on numerous occasions over the centuries, each ruler leaving his mark. The line-up of statues along the facade – the eight dynasties that ruled Naples from Roger the Norman to Victor Emmanuel of Savoy – present a potted history of the city.

Inside, a majestic double staircase ascends to the **royal apartments**, resplendent with Baroque and neoclassical paintings, sculpture, tapestries and porcelain. The highlights are the ornate **Court Theatre** (1768; closed for restoration at the time of writing) and the **Royal Chapel**, which has a magnificent altar by Lazzari (1674), master of Neapolitan Baroque decoration, and a vast *presepe* (Christmas crib). The palace

is also home to the **Biblioteca Nazionale** (Mon–Fri 8.30am–7.30pm, Sat 8.30am–1.30pm); its vast collection of books and manuscripts includes some 2,000 parchments from Herculaneum. The palace's hanging gardens are closed for restoration, but the garden to the left of the main entrance leads to another lovely one with views of the bay.

SANTA LUCIA

Exit the square on Via Cesario Console, then turn right into **Via Santa Lucia ❼**, which cuts through the old fishermen's quarter and leads down to the sea. Rising above it to the right is the **Pizzofalcone** hill, site of the Greek settlement of Parthenope that predated Neapolis by three centuries.

Luxury hotels hog all the best views along Via Partenope, the road that skirts the bay, with the most exclusive promising direct views of Castel dell'Ovo. Nestled in the tiny harbour at the foot of the castle is the **Borgo Marinaro ❽**, an atmospheric enclave of seafood restaurants, romantically candlelit after dark, or a stunning spot for lunch, surrounded by bobbing fishing boats. Stop at **La Scialuppa**, see ⑪②, or next-door **Antica Trattoria da Pietro**, see ⑪③, for a fish feast.

Castel dell'Ovo
The **Castel dell'Ovo ❾** (tel: 081-240 0055; Mon–Sat 9am–6pm, Sun 9am–2pm; free) is the oldest castle in

---

Musica Napoletana

Traditional Neapolitan music is a deeply rooted part of the city's culture: wander down any *centro storico* back alley and you're almost bound to hear a serenade being warbled through an open window. The *canzone napoletana* became a formally recognised genre in the 1830s, thanks to the Festival of Piedigrotta, a local songwriting competition. It petered out in the 1950s, but classics such as *Funiculì, Funiculà* and *O Sole Mio* remain as popular as ever. At the Raccolta de Mura (tel: 081-420 3331; Mon–Sat 9am–6pm, Sun 9am–1pm; free), hidden away under Piazza Trieste e Trento (take the flight of steps next to Bar del Professore), you can browse through a painstakingly assembled private collection of vintage festival programmes, posters and sheet music, to the cheery soundtrack of Neapolitan classics.

Naples. It occupies a tiny islet named Megaris by the Greeks, who used it as a harbour.

The original fortress was built by the Aragonese in the 12th century, but most of the present structure dates from the early 16th century, when the citadel was rebuilt following its near destruction by the Spanish. Today, the castle is used to host cultural events and exhibitions, but the real appeal is pottering around on the battlements and gazing at the views.

THE LUNGOMARE

The broad stretch of road that sweeps around the bay from the castle, past the Villa Comunale *(see p.43)* to Mergellina, is punctuated at each end by a 17th-century fountain. A stroll along the seafront, or **Lungomare** ❿, with an ice cream in hand, is a Neapolitan Sunday ritual.

Look out for the padlocks on the railings along this stretch – part of an Italy-wide craze that sees amorous teenagers 'locking' their love to public monuments.

CHIAIA

Continue along Via Partenope until you reach the park, then turn right into **Piazza Vittoria** ⓫ and follow boutique-lined Via Calabritto to **Piazza dei Martiri** ⓬, the epicentre of chichi Chiaia *(see also p.40)*. Take

the next left on to Via Alabardieri to reach **Enoteca Belledonne**, see ⑪④, the perfect place for an *aperitivo*, before wandering back to Piazza Plebiscito along pedestrianised **Via Chiaia** ⓭, favoured by Naples' best-dressed for their evening *passeggiata*. All along this stretch, cocktail bars fizz with early-evening chatter, and Chiaia's well-heeled residents pose, flirt and people-watch as they gear up for the night ahead.

Above from far left: Castel dell'Ovo; the fortress occupies the islet of Megaris; a Via Chiaia balcony.

Food and Drink

② LA SCIALUPPA

Borgo Marinaro 4; tel: 081-764 5333; www.lascialuppa.it; daily 12.30–3pm, 7–10.30pm, closed Tue in May; €€€
Bag a table on the flower-filled terrace or soak up the atmosphere in the dining room, with huge windows overlooking the Borgo Marinaro and a riot of nautical knick-knacks. Fish is the speciality and it can be pricey, but you can order a pizza and enjoy the same views for a fraction of the price.

③ ANTICA TRATTORIA DA PIETRO

Via Luculliana 27; tel: 347-705 9656; daily 12.30–3pm, 7.30–10.30pm; €€
A refreshingly honestly priced option for the Borgo Marinaro, with a handful of outdoor tables on the waterfront. The *gnocchetti di Pietro*, with calamari and olives, makes a delicious *primo*; follow with the daily fish special.

④ ENOTECA BELLEDONNE

Via Belledonne a Chiaia 18; tel: 081-403 162; www.enoteca belledonne.com; daily 10am–1.30pm, 5pm–midnight, Fri–Sat until 2am, in summer opens 7pm on Mon; €
The early-evening crowds at this hugely popular wine bar shun the handful of tables in favour of the cobbled street outside. Come between 7pm and 10pm or after midnight for the best atmosphere – or outside of these times if you're after a quiet drink. The wine list is extensive, with lots of options by the glass, served with deliciously salty *taralli* pastries.

CHIAIA AND VOMERO

A full day exploring the well-heeled and pleasantly airy districts of Chiaia, with its uptown shopping, and Vomero, full of knockout views, culminating in a stroll along the seafront to lively Mergellina.

DISTANCE 6km (3¾ miles)
TIME A full day
START Piazza dei Martiri
END Mergellina
POINTS TO NOTE

This is a good walk to do with children. Book restaurants in advance, especially at weekends.

PAN

The Palazzo delle Arti di Napoli – or PAN for short – at 60 Via dei Mille (tel: 081-795 8605; www.palazzo artinapoli.net; Mon–Sat 9.30am–7.30pm, Sun 9.30am–2.30pm; charge for exhibitions) is a must for contemporary-art lovers. There's usually an interesting exhibition on – from sculpture to photography, video art to comics – and there's a great shop too, with lots of offbeat, arty gift ideas.

After spending time in the crowded *centro storico*, the spacious, elegant districts of Chiaia and Vomero – the former all chichi boutiques, the latter airy boulevards – offer welcome breathing space. Chiaia became fashionable in the 19th century, when Naples' popularity among the European elite increased, and it remains a pocket of privilege from which its impeccably attired residents rarely stray. The Vomero hill above was just a sleepy village until the turn of the century. The building of elegant neo-Renaissance *palazzi* attracted wealthy Neapolitans, and after World War II, unregulated building covered most of the hill with modern blocks. Traces of its aristocratic past endure, however, in its spacious avenues and the few handsome buildings that were spared.

CHIAIA

Start at **Piazza dei Martiri ❶**, Chiaia's lively hub. The column at its centre commemorates those who died in the anti-Bourbon revolutions. Head north out of the square, veering left into **Via G. Filangieri ❷**, which becomes Via dei Mille. Both streets are lined with exclusive shops and designer boutiques, with stately *palazzi* in between. The network of streets between this stretch and the Riviera di Chiaia yields more boutiques – Via della Cavallerizza and Via Poerio are particularly good. Via dei Mille runs into Via Vittoria Colonna, which ends at **Piazza Amedeo ❸**. The road to the right of the metro station here leads to the **funicular ❹**, which whisks you up to Vomero; get off at the last stop, **Cimarosa ❺**.

VILLA FLORIDIANA

Turn left out of the funicular station and walk along Via Cimarosa until you reach the **Villa Floridiana ❻** (8.30am–1hr before sunset; free). Paths lined with benches wind past densely planted shrubbery, opening out on to a sloping lawn – a favourite local picnic

spot – and the Villa Floridiana itself. Once described as a 'Baroque chocolate box with neoclassical touches', it was originally a wedding present from King Ferdinand I to Lucia Migliaccio, his morganatic wife.

Museo Nazionale di Ceramica

The villa now houses the **Museo Nazionale di Ceramica Duca di Martina ⑦** (tel: 081-229 2110; Wed–Mon 8.30am–2pm, ticket office shuts 45 mins before closing; charge), with one of Italy's finest collections of fine china, including 18th-century porcelain from Meissen, Limoges, Sèvres and nearby Capodimonte. The oriental collection in the basement is the museum's greatest treasure, with Chinese and Japanese ceramics gathered in the 19th century by the museum's namesake, the Duke of Martina. Before leaving Villa Floridiana, walk round the back through the gardens

Above from far left: handsome buildings on the Riviera di Chiaia; Villa Floridiana, which houses the Museo Nazionale di Ceramica Duca di Martina.

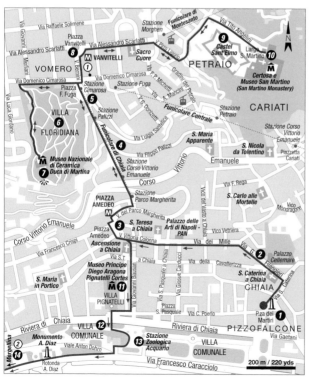

Chiaia's *Pasticcerie*

Chiaia has an abundance of tempting pastry shops, or *pasticcerie*, that will package up your purchases in dainty little parcels. Among the best are Gran Bar Riviera (Riviera di Chiaia 183), which specialises in *crostata di fragole*, a pastry tart loaded with mini strawberries; Gran Caffè Cimmino (Via Filangieri 12–13), a favourite coffee spot selling super-sized *babà*; and Moccia (Via San Pasquale a Chiaia 21–22), specialising in *mignon* (bite-sized pastry treats) and handmade chocolates.

Above from left:
the glorious view from
the Castel Sant'Elmo;
opulent Villa Pignatelli;
the port of Mergellina.

to the viewing platform at the bottom, which offers panoramic views of the city and the bay.

Back at the park gates, turn right along Via Cimarosa and stop at **Acunzo**, see ⑪①, for a hearty lunch. Backtrack to the funicular and take Via Bernini, leading off it, to bustling **Piazza Vanvitelli ❽**.

CASTEL SANT'ELMO

Take Via Alessandro Scarlatti, which leads off Piazza Vanvitelli to the right, climbing the two flights of steps up to the funicular station. Follow the road round to the right for the hulking **Castel Sant'Elmo ❾** (entrance at Via Tito Angelini 20; tel: 081-578 4030; Wed–Mon 8.30am–7.30pm, last entry 6.30pm; charge). Construction of the fortress was begun in 1329 by Robert of Anjou; in the mid-16th century, Spanish viceroy Don Pedro de Toledo added the six-pointed star shape, making the castle virtually impregnable. But in 1587 disaster struck when an explosion in the powder magazine all but destroyed it. The castle was gradually rebuilt and for many years served as a dungeon. Today the interior is used for exhibitions, but the main reason for visiting is to enjoy the staggering 360° view of the city from its battlements.

Back at the gate, turn right, pausing to admire the palazzo at no. 41, resplendent with nautical motifs, before continuing to the San Martino Monastery.

SAN MARTINO MONASTERY

Sharing the castle's hilltop perch is the **San Martino Monastery ❿** (Piazzale San Martino 5; tel: 081-558 6408; Thur–Tue 8.30am–7.30pm, Sun 9am–7.30pm; last entry 6.30pm; charge), founded in 1325 but worked on by different artists in the 17th century.

Cosimo Fanzago expanded the original Angevin **church**, giving it a Baroque makeover. He added a new facade and had the interior lavishly decorated with coloured marble and paintings by the masters of Neapolitan Baroque: Massimo Stanzione, Giuseppe Ribera, Francesco Solimena and Giovanni Lanfranco. The intricate marble balustrade in front of the altar (18th century) is by Giuseppe Sammartino.

A door at the back of the church leads to the **sacristy and chapter room**, with inlaid walnut panelling. You emerge from these sombre rooms into the bright **Chiostro Grande**, enclosed by a 64-column arcade of grey and white marble and a monks' graveyard, watched over by an eerie set of skulls ranged along a balustrade.

The **art gallery** is spread across two floors, its rooms facing on to the cloister on one side and offering more fantastic views of Naples on the other. Most of the 17th- and 18th-century works are housed in the former prior's quarters. Among the fine maps and landscapes, look out for the earliest pictorial record

Take the Stairs
Before Vomero's
funiculars were
installed in the late
19th and early 20th
centuries, the only way
up from the city centre
was the knee-
trembling climb up
long flights of steps.
Forgoing the funicular
to take the steps
down is a little
arduous but at least
allows you to enjoy the
view. Via Pedamentina
di San Martino is the
most rewarding path
(though uneven, so
watch your step); it
starts opposite the
monastery and zig-
zags downhill to Corso
Vittorio Emanuele.

of Naples, the **Tavola Strozzi** (1465), showing the original monastery atop Vomero hill. One of the museum's prize exhibits is the **Presepe Napoletano**, a vast 18th-century crib populated with scores of terracotta figures.

Backtrack to the Cimarosa funicular and return to Chiaia.

VILLA PIGNATELLI

From Piazza Amadeo, take Via Vittoria Colonna and turn right down the steps for **Villa Pignatelli ⑪** (Via della Riviera di Chiaia 200; tel: 081-761 2356; Wed–Mon 8.30am–1pm; charge). The neoclassical villa was built in 1826 for Ferdinand Acton, son of Ferdinand IV's prime minister. It was bought in 1841 by the Rothschilds, who sold it to the noble Pignatelli Cortes family. The ground floor has a ballroom, a library, and fine porcelain and paintings.

VILLA COMUNALE

Crossing traffic-choked Riviera di Chiaia to the **Villa Comunale ⑫**, it's hard to imagine a time when this was a peaceful residential area. King Ferdinand IV cleared a block of buildings along here to turn his favourite strolling ground into a public park filled with exotic plants. On Sunday afternoons the park is full of smartly dressed families parading under the shady palms.

The **Stazione Zoologica Acquario ⑬** (Aquarium; tel: 081-583 3263; www.

szn.it; summer: Tue–Sat 9am–6pm, Sun 9.30am–7.30pm; winter Tue–Sat 9am–5pm, Sun 9am–2pm; charge) is Europe's oldest aquarium: built in 1874, it still contains the original 23 tanks. Peer into the murky depths at the variety of indigenous species that survive in the polluted waters of the bay.

MERGELLINA

Exit the park and follow Via Caracciolo west along the seafront to the port of **Mergellina ⑭**. On the opposite side of the marina is a line-up of scruffy kiosks – or 'chalets' – selling drinks and snacks. **Chalet Ciro**, see ⑪②, is perfectly placed for an ice cream as you ogle the yachts in the harbour.

Antiques Market

During the Fiera Antiquaria Napoletana (www.fieraantiquaria napoletana.it), antiques sellers set up their wares between the Villa Comunale and Via Caracciolo on the waterfront, selling anything from old armoires to Christmas crib figurines. The market takes place on the third Sunday of the month and the preceding Saturday (except Aug) and the fourth Sunday of the month and preceding Saturday (except Jun–Aug), from 8am to 2pm.

Food and Drink

① ACUNZO
Via Cimarosa 60; tel: 081-578 5362; Mon-Sat 1–3pm, 7.30–11.30pm; €

The closely packed tables at this unpretentious little trattoria are taken up by hungry local workers, or at weekends by local families enjoying huge plates of pasta and generous pizzas; the house special is topped with sausage, *friarelli* (local greens), peppers, aubergine and cheese. No bookings on Saturdays.

② CHALET CIRO
Via Caracciolo 31; tel: 081-669 928; www.chaletciro.it; Mon, Tue, Thur–Sun 7am–3am; €

Brace yourself for queue-barging and general confusion at the legendary Chalet Ciro: for ice cream this good, the locals don't like to wait in line. The pastries are excellent too, or combine the two: a *gelato-* and cream-stuffed brioche here is a classic way to end the Sunday-afternoon seafront stroll so beloved of Neapolitans.

THE CATACOMBS
AND MUSEUMS

This full-day tour explores the artistic and archaeological treasures of Naples' top two museums, and takes in some more offbeat sights en route, most notably one of the area's subterranean cemeteries and the engagingly untouristic district of La Sanità.

DISTANCE 2.5km (1½ miles)
TIME A full day
START Museo di Capodimonte
END Museo Archeologico Nazionale
POINTS TO NOTE
To get to the Museo di Capodimonte take bus R4 or C63 from the port or Piazza Dante, or bus 178, M2 or 201 from Piazza Museo. You will need at least three hours for each museum, but the tour can easily be split up. The opening hours of the catacombs require you to set out early – a 9am start will allow you to see the Museo di Capodimonte first. Take an extra layer of clothing for the catacombs as they can be chilly, and keep a close eye on your belongings in La Sanità. The Museo Archeologico is part of a cumulative Campi Flegrei ticket (€8.50; valid three days), which includes the Museo Archeologico at Báia, the Anfiteatro Flavio at Pozzuoli and Cuma *(see tour 5)*.

Sightseeing Shuttle
A shuttle bus service run by City Sightseeing (www.napoli.city-sightseeing.it) starts in Largo Castello next to Piazza Municipio and runs to the Museo di Capodimonte every 90 minutes from 9.30am to 6.30pm, taking in the Duomo, M.A.D.RE and the Museo Archeologico en route. Tickets are €3 for a single trip, €8 for a day ticket, or free with the Campania Artecard *(see p.11)*.

When the noise and chaos of the city get too much for you, head for Naples' top two museums – the Museo di Capodimonte and the Museo Archeologico – whose well-presented collections rival those at Europe's best museums. Between the two are a number of lesser-known sights, equally rewarding in their own way: the fascinating Catacombs of San Gaudioso and the workaday district of La Sanità.

MUSEO DI CAPODIMONTE

The **Museo di Capodimonte** ❶ (tel: 081-749 9111; www.museo-capodimonte.it; Thur–Tue 8.30am–7.30pm; charge), one of Italy's finest art museums, sits in the hilltop haven of Capodimonte, in its own well-tended park. When he became king, Charles III of Bourbon gathered all the artworks he had inherited from his mother, Elisabetta Farnese, to Naples. The problem was where to house them. While on one of his hunting trips, the king decided that the hill to the north

of the city, with its commanding views of the bay and game-filled woods, was the perfect site for a hunting lodge and royal residence that would double as a museum for his precious collection. Building began in 1738, but progress was slow: the three-storey palace took 100 years to complete.

The core Farnese collection, rich in Renaissance art, was augmented by the Bourbon collection and subsequent acquisitions, many from churches and convents in the area. The collection now runs the gamut from Byzantine panel painting to contemporary art installations.

Farnese Gallery

The visit begins with the **Farnese Gallery** on the first floor. The collection features some important early works – Masaccio's *Crucifixion*, a Botticelli Madonna and Filippino Lippi's *Annunciation and Saints* – but the 16th-century paintings are the cream of the crop. Highlights include *Antea* by Parmigianino, the portrait of an elegantly dressed young woman thought to be the artist's lover, and the monumental canvases by the Carraccis. The influence of Michelangelo is evident in the sculpted figures of Annibale Carracci's *Pietà* and in his *Hercules at the Crossroads*. Raphael is a dominant presence with his portraits of *Leo X and Two Cardinals* and *Cardinal Alessandro Farnese*. Pride of place is given to Titian's *Danaë*, which represents

the mythical love scene from Ovid's *Metamorphoses* in which Zeus disguises himself as a shower of gold in order to seduce Danaë, daughter of the king of Argos. In the same room is *El Soflon* by El Greco, a mesmerising study of young boy blowing on a burning coal.

Above: the imposing exterior and lovely gardens of the Museo di Capodimonte.

LUCAN
LIBRARY
TEL. 6216422

Above from far left:
Caravaggio's
Flagellation; Warhol's
Vesuvius; inside a La
Sanità church.

Galleria delle Cose Rare

The **Galleria delle Cose Rare** contains a sparkling display of rare and precious objects that once graced the Farnese palaces. The rooms beyond are taken up by Flemish paintings, mostly acquired by the Bourbons at the beginning of the 17th century, a mix of earthy, pastoral scenes and still lifes.

Royal Apartments

Before heading up to the second floor, wander through the ornate **Royal Apartments** and marvel at the magnificent ballroom with its giant chandelier, and the Porcelain Parlour of Queen Maria Amalia, lined with over 3,000 tiles made in King Charles's porcelain factory.

Second Floor

The second floor is given over to Neapolitan art from the 13th–18th centuries. Among the early works is Simone Martini's *San Ludovico di Tolosa*, a masterpiece of Italian Gothic art from San Lorenzo Maggiore. Central to the 17th-century works in the collection are the Caravaggio canvases, in particular the *Flagellation*, which was transferred from San Domenico Maggiore. This influential painting heralded a golden age of Neapolitan art, whose leading lights were Mattia Preti, Giuseppe de Ribera, Battistello Caracciolo and Luca Giordano, all represented. Don't miss the monumental d'Avalos tapestries, made in Brussels

for the Habsburg emperor Charles V, to commemorate his victory over the French in the Battle of Pavia.

The gallery's modern-art collection starts on the second floor with Alberto Burri's *Grande Cretto Nero*.

Third Floor

The third floor and part of the former attics are dedicated to modern and contemporary art. Don't miss the star exhibit, Andy Warhol's iconic *Vesuvius*. Before leaving, browse in the prints and drawings gallery on the ground floor. Its 27,500-strong collection includes cartoons by Raphael and Michelangelo, and prints by, among others, Dürer and Rembrandt.

There's more contemporary art in the **Sala Causa**, off the courtyard, which holds big-name temporary exhibitions.

Parco di Capodimonte

Revive yourself with a coffee in the courtyard café, then take a stroll around the **Parco di Capodimonte** *(see margin, left)*.

Take bus C63, 178 or 2M from almost opposite the entrance to the park and get off at the first stop after you pass the green-and-yellow tiled cupola on your left (or it's a 25-minute walk down the twisting road). Here you'll find a lift *(ascensore)* down to the district of La Sanità and, beneath the imposing grey church of Santa Maria della Sanità, the Catacombs of San Gaudioso.

Parco di Capodimonte
The gardens were laid out in 1742 by architect Sanfelice, whose designs were influenced both by the formal French style and the Romantic English style. Sanfelice was also commissioned to build the royal porcelain factory, which turned out top-quality porcelain until Charles dismantled the operation and transferred it, workers and all, to Spain when he returned there in 1759.

CATACOMBE DI SAN GAUDIOSO

The area beneath the park and down towards the workaday district of La Sanità is honeycombed with catacombs; a visit to one of these subterranean cemeteries is an unmissable experience.

First tunnelled out of the rock by the Ancient Romans, who used them as water cisterns, the **Catacombe di San Gaudioso ②** (14 Piazza della Sanità; tel: 081-544 1305; www.catacombedi napoli.it; daily 10am–1pm, hour-long guided tours only every hour, call to request a tour in English; charge) were used as Christian burial sites from the 5th century onwards. Through the musty gloom you can still make out remnants of 5th- and 6th-century mosaics and faded frescoes: look out for the Christian symbols of the lamb, the peacock, and the bunch of grapes. Skulls are set into niches above frescoed portraits of their bodies, revealing their owners' professions, such as the robes of a judge and a knight's sword.

LA SANITÀ

Back above ground, explore **La Sanità**, one of Naples' most characterful districts: untouched by tourism, this appealingly rowdy network of streets is a great place to absorb yourself in the sights and sounds of the city. Follow **Via della Sanità ③** from the church. Full of the chaotic energy

that characterises Naples and buzzing at all hours with locals going about their daily business, this crowded stretch offers as authentic a slice of Neapolitan life as you'll find anywhere in the city. The area is peppered with Catholic shrines – stop at Traversa Lammatari and look to your right for a typically overblown example.

Via delle Vergini

Just before the road veers left, peek into the courtyard of the **Palazzo Sanfelice ④** to your right to admire its magnificent – though sadly dilapidated – double staircases. Via della Sanità merges with **Via delle Vergini ⑤**, site of a colourful local market (daily 8am–8pm), selling everything from flowers to frying pans. No. 19, **Palazzo dello Spagnuolo ⑥**, holds another impressive double staircase, this one newly restored. A small museum on the top floor is dedicated to Totò, veteran comic actor and the area's most famous son.

Catacombe di San Gennaro
Your catacombs ticket also gets you entry to the two-level Catacombe di San Gennaro, at Via Tondo di Capodimonte 13 (guided tours only; hourly Tue–Sat 10am–7pm, Sun 10am–1pm; charge), which are embellished with 2nd-century frescoes.

Below: stairway in the Palazzo Sanfelice.

Above from far left: exhibits at the Museo Archeologico.

Turn right off Via delle Vergini on to cobbled Via Misericordiella and stop for lunch at **O'Core 'e Napule**, see ⑪①, or, further along the street, have a snack at **Mignone**, see ⑪②, before moving on to the Museo Archeologico.

MUSEO ARCHEOLOGICO

At the far end of Piazza Cavour, the **Museo Archeologico Nazionale ❼** (National Archeological Museum; Piazza Museo 19; tel: 081-442 2149; http://museoarcheologiconazionale. campaniabeniculturali.it; Wed–Mon 9am–7.30pm; charge) is an unparalleled collection of Greek and Roman artefacts. The museum occupies a hulking red *palazzo* on the northern outskirts of the *centro storico*. Originally the seat of Naples University, the 17th-century building was requisitioned in 1777 by Ferdinand IV to house the Farnese collection bequeathed to him by his father, Charles III of Bourbon. Charles's mother came from the aristocratic Farnese family whose members had assembled a vast collection of antique and contemporary art. Ferdinand wanted to gather as much of the scattered collection as he could under one roof with the aim of establishing a 'temple of wisdom and knowledge'.

Farnese Collection

The Farnese collection of antiquities is spread across the ground floor. Many of the sculptures are in fact Roman copies of Greek masterpieces. The Farnese *Hercules* in the main gallery is a first-rate copy of a statue by the Greek master Lysippus. At the opposite end stands the *Farnese Bull* (*c.*200BC), a monumental sculpture carved from a single block of marble. It depicts the death of Dirce, tied to a bull by Antiope's sons for the attempted murder of their mother. Both magnificent statues come from the Baths of Caracalla in Rome. Other highlights are the *Aphrodite Callipige*, admiring the reflection of her curvaceous rear; the bronze and

Food and Drink

① O' CORE 'E NAPULE
Via Misericordiella 23–24; tel: 081-292 566; www.ocoree napule.com; daily noon–midnight; €€
With a handful of outdoor tables and a bustling dining room, this trattoria is hugely popular with locals. The excellent pizzas are the main draw here, especially the calzone-style Tronchetto, topped with prosciutto, rocket and Parmesan, with a melting centre of Emmenthal and mozzarella. Come hungry.

② MIGNONE
Piazza Cavour 146; tel: 081-293 074; Tue–Sun 7.30am–8pm; €
This hole-in-the-wall *pasticceria* has all the Neapolitan classics – *babà, pastiera, sfogliatelle* – as well as gourmet chocolates. Perfect for a sugar hit before the Museo Archeologico.

③ OSTERIA DA CARMELA
Via Conte di Ruvo 11–12; tel: 081-549 9738; Mon–Sat noon–3.30pm, 7pm–1am; €€
A meal at this homely one-room *osteria*, with doily-covered tables and family paintings on the walls, feels somewhat like dinner at your elderly aunt's house. The menu is equally lacking in pretension, with a handful of simple *primi* and *secondi*. It's cheaper at lunch, with mains at just €6.

alabaster *Artemis of Ephesus*; and the *Tyrannicides*, another masterly copy of a 4th-century Greek original.

Leading off the main gallery is a room full of incised gems and intricate cameos. The prize piece here is the *Tazza Farnese*, a fragile Egyptian dish of sardonyx agate, which has among the spoils of war brought to Rome by Octavian after his victory over Cleopatra. In the basement is the museum's small Egyptian collection, part of which came from the Borgia family (closed for restoration at the time of writing).

Mosaics Collection

The mezzanine floor is shared between a 200,000-strong coin collection on one side, and Roman mosaics and the 'secret room' of Pompeiian erotica on the other. The finest mosaics come from the houses of wealthy Pompeiians, most notably the House of the Faun (named after the lovely bronze sculpture of a dancing faun, displayed on the first floor). The undisputed masterpiece here is the mosaic of the Battle of Issus, depicting Alexander the Great's victory over the Persian king Darius. Animals were a favourite theme and there are realistic portrayals of cats and dogs, exotic creatures from the Nile and marine life.

Gabinetto Segreto

The so-called **Gabinetto Segreto** is the biggest draw. Until recently, the statuettes, reliefs, mosaics and frescoes displayed here were deemed too pornographic for public viewing; the entrance to the secret room is still manned to prevent under-12s from going in. The explicit images of sexual antics between men, women, nymphs, satyrs and, in one case, a god and a goat, will leave you in no doubt as to the Roman taste for eroticism. Phalluses abound in every shape and form; as well as symbolising virility and fertility, they were used as good-luck charms to ward off the evil eye.

First Floor

All the rooms on the first floor lead off the central **Salone Meridiana**, a vast hall decorated with frescoes and paintings glorifying the Bourbon dynasty *(see margin, right)*. Most of this floor is dedicated to the Vesuvian paintings, as well as items from Paestum and other sites of Magna Grecia. Highlights also include the 118-piece silver collection from the Casa del Menandro, part of a hoard found in a wooden chest together with gold jewellery, precious stones and silver and gold coins; the famous Blue Vase, a glass-cameo amphora from Pompeii; and a series of rooms containing bronze statues and a wealth of other finds from the **Villa dei Papiri** in Herculaneum *(see p.59)*.

If the day's sightseeing has given you a healthy appetite, head to **Osteria Da Carmela**, see ①③, a short stroll south along Via Santa Maria di Costantinopoli.

Salone Meridiana
Set into the floor of the Salone Meridiana is a meridian line decorated at calculated intervals with signs of the zodiac. At midday a shaft of light falls from a hole in the top right-hand corner of the room and hits the sign that corresponds to the time of year.

Below: sculptures at the museum.

THE CAMPI FLEGREI

This tour covers the little-explored but fascinating Phlegraean Fields.
Mythologised by the ancients as the entrance to the Underworld, this area
of geological quirks and archaeological wonders makes for a rewarding
daytrip from Naples.

DISTANCE 4km (2½ miles) on
foot plus 20km (12½ miles)
driving or on public transport
TIME A full day
START Pozzuoli
END Cuma
POINTS TO NOTE
The Campi Flegrei are not well connected by public transport, though
all sights are served by buses and
trains. A boat service runs from
Molo Beverello to the Campi Flegrei
twice daily in summer (www.metro
delmare.net). By car, take the Tan-
genziale (ring road) west from
Naples through Fuorigrotta; exits
are marked. By public transport,
take a train from Naples' Montesanto station to Pozzuoli on the
Cumana line. From the Lucrino
stop on the same line take a bus to
Baia. EAV buses run from Báia to
the Cumana station at Fusaro,
where you can change for a bus to
Cuma. Ferries run to Pozzuoli from
Ischia and Procida (tours 11 and
12). The ground is uneven at Solfatara, so wear appropriate footwear.

Joint Tickets
One of the Artecard
tourist passes (*see*
p.11), 'Napoli e Campi
Flegrei', gives you
access to the first
three sights and half-
price entrance to the
rest for €16 (valid for
three days), including
transport. Participating
sights include all of the
places on this tour,
plus many of Naples'
major museums.
Alternatively, a €4
ticket will get you into
the archaeological
museum at Báia,
Cuma and the
Anfiteatro Flavio.

The area west of Naples, between
Pozzuoli and Cuma, is known as the
Campi Flegrei (Phlegraean Fields),
from the Greek *fleguròs* meaning fire.
Back in the 8th century BC, when the
first Greek colonists settled in Cuma,
the volcanic terrain bubbled and hissed
with the activity of some 20 now-
extinct craters. Its ghostly atmosphere
led the ancients to believe this was the
gateway of the dead, and inspired both
Virgil and Dante to create their vision
of hell. But such sinister associations
didn't deter the Romans, who were
drawn by the fertile land, mild climate
and hot springs, and built luxurious
villas and spas all along the coast.

By the 1st century AD, the Campi
Flegrei was one of the empire's most
fashionable resorts, frequented by rich
merchants, poets, philosophers, gen-
erals and emperors – a far cry from
its somewhat neglected modern-day
incarnation: the Greco-Roman ruins
lie buried under a sea of concrete.
Picturesque it isn't, but ancient history
still oozes from every street, port and
hillside, and it is so far off the tourist
trail that you may well find that you
have the sights to yourself.

POZZUOLI

The starting point of this itinerary is the port of **Pozzuoli ❶**, which has three claims to fame: its Greco-Roman remains, its active crater and the fact that it is the birthplace of Sophia Loren. There's a lot of ground to cover, so get here as early as you can.

Tempio di Serapide

The Cumana train drops you near the port; evidence of the Roman colony of Puteoli is visible all over town. Turn right from the station to reach the 1st-century market, or **Tempio di Serapide**, on the seafront, which was submerged in water until 1985 when the effects of bradyseism – the rising and falling of land levels caused by volcanic activity – left it uncovered. Note the perforations on the columns, made by molluscs during its long existence under water.

Rione Terra

Backtrack to the station and take Via G. De Fraia to your left to get to the centre, then turn left and walk up the hill for the **Rione Terra** excavations (closed at the time of writing, but usually open Sat–Sun; charge). These have uncovered a once-thriving ancient town, with remains of an Augustan temple, a bakery, a mill and slave lodgings.

Head back downhill to the port – if you want to eat lunch in Pozzuoli, this is

Above from far left: Pozzuoli's Tempio di Serapide; a fisherman in the harbour.

Above: quiet corners in Pozzuoli.

The Anfiteatro and San Gennaro
According to legend, the amphitheatre has survived almost intact thanks to the piety of Pozzuoli's citizens, who commemorated it as the place where San Gennaro was imprisoned before being beheaded at the Solfatara, AD305.

Above from left:
the bubbling Solfatara;
view from the Castello
di Báia; Cuma's Cave
of the Sibyl.

Hot and Steamy
A 2009 American
study investigating an
unusual number of
large families in the
Pozzuoli area revealed
a link between the
Solfatara's sulphurous
gases and male virility.
After the results
were published, the
attraction recorded
an increase in
visitor numbers.

the place. Join the throng on the esplanade, and walk to the end of the port to reach **Grottino a' Mmare**, see ①①. For a snack, head to **Caffè Serapide**, see ①②, in the central Piazza Repubblica.

Anfiteatro Flavio

Bus 152 runs from the opposite side of the piazza from the station to the **Anfiteatro Flavio ②** (Via Terracciano 75; tel: 848-800 288; Wed–Mon 9am–1hr before sunset; ticket office closes 1hr earlier; charge). This well-preserved amphitheatre held 40,000 spectators and was the third largest in the ancient world; fragments of columns and statuary scattered across the site are reminders of what it once was. Concerts are held here from June to September.

Solfatara

Bus 152 continues uphill to the **Solfatara ③** (Via Solfatara 161; daily 8.30am–7pm; charge), a partially active crater in a strikingly lunar landscape. Volcanic activity is much more subdued since the crater was formed in 2000BC,

Right: beach at Báia.

but you can still feel the heat, smell the pungent sulphur and get up close to the fumaroles, gas jets and bubbling mud.

Buses P9 and 152 run back down to the Cumana station, where you can take a train to Lucrino, then a bus to Báia.

BÁIA

Traces of an old Roman baths complex and adjacent temples are scattered along the **Port of Báia ④**, but you need to stretch your imagination to see this nondescript town as the luxurious spa it was. Much of the ancient resort now lies under the sea due to bradyseism *(see p.51)*. In the area are some good restaurants; try **Il Tucano**, see ①③, or **La Tortuga**, see ①④, next door.

Castello di Báia

The road out of the port winds round to Báia's main attraction, the **Castello di Báia ⑤** (Tue–Sun 9am–1hr before sunset; charge), sitting in splendid isolation at the tip of the headland, overlooking the Gulf of Pozzuoli. Built by the Aragonese, it was restructured by Don Pedro de Toledo after the 1538 eruption. Despite being expensively revamped in 2008, all but one of the archaeological museum's rooms are closed until further notice. The Sala Rione Terra has sculptures unearthed in Pozzuoli; when the museum fully opens, it should be possible to visit the impressive collection of archaeological treasures from all over the region.

Buses run from Báia to Bacoli; ask the driver where to get off for the **Piscina Mirabilis**. Ring the bell at the custodian's house on the corner of Via Piscina Mirabilis for access (daily 9am–1.30pm, 2.30–6.45pm; free). This immense cistern, carved out of the volcanic rock and supported by 48 pillars, held enough water to supply the entire Roman fleet anchored at Miseno.

CUMA

From Bacoli or Báia get an EAV bus to Fusaro's Cumana station, and change for a bus to Cuma. From where the bus stops, walk up the hill to the **Archaeological Park** (Tue–Sun 9am–1hr before sunset; charge) containing remains of the ancient Roman bath complex.

The main archaeological site of **Cuma** ❻ (9am–1hr before sunset; charge) is a little further up the hill. The first colony of Magna Grecia, it was founded in the 8th century BC by Greek traders based in Ischia. It's easy to understand why they chose to abandon their volcanically active island in favour of such a well-positioned and fertile headland. The finest sight is the Cave of the Sibyl, a long, echoing trapezoid corridor carved into the hill of the acropolis, pierced by shafts of light that fall through side openings, creating an ethereal semi-darkness. Legend has it that this was the domain of the sibyl, the prophetess in Virgil's *Aeneid* who guided Aeneas through the Underworld and predicted the fall of Rome. Steps lead up to the ruins of the **Temple of Apollo** and, higher still, the **Temple of Jupiter**, an ancient Greek sanctuary later transformed into a Christian church. It's worth the climb for sweeping views over the surrounding woodland.

Buses run from the site to Fusaro Cumana station, from where you can take a train back to Naples.

Underwater Villas

At weekends in summer, glass-bottomed boats ferry tourists from the port of Báia to the fascinating ruined villas under the water. Booking is obligatory on tel: 349-497 4183, or prenotazioni@ baiasommersa.it.

Food and Drink

① GROTTINO A'MMARE

Via dell'Emporio 35–37, Pozzuoli; tel: 081-526 2480; www.grottinoammare.it; Tue–Sun noon–3.30pm, 7pm–1am; €€€
A smart choice, with simple, elegant table settings on a decked terrace overlooking the water. The restaurant has been serving up the freshest of the day's catch since 1912; the *pezzogna* fish is the one to go for.

② CAFFÈ SERAPIDE

Piazza della Repubblica 94, Pozzuoli; tel: 081-806 0183; www.caffeserapide.it; 24hr daily; €
A good menu of light meals – omelettes, salads and panini – and tables on a flower-filled terrace right on the central square. There are also excellent pastries and ice cream if you just want a quick snack.

③ IL TUCANO

Via Molo di Baia 40, Báia; tel: 081-854 5046; www.iltucano.net; Tue–Sun 12.30–3pm, 7.30pm–midnight; €
Pizza (sold by the metre), big salads and snacks are the order of the day at this informal restaurant, with its buzzy open terrace. There's also a small daily menu of pastas and *secondi* if you want a full meal. Bookings taken for lunch only.

④ LA TORTUGA

Via Molo di Baia 42, Báia; tel: 081-868 8878; www.la tortugaportodibaia.com; daily 12.45–4pm, 7.30pm–midnight, closed Tue in winter; €€€
Linen-covered tables and a smartly dressed clientele set the tone at this elegant restaurant in Báia's port. There's no menu: dishes change daily depending on the day's catch.

POMPEII, VESUVIUS AND HERCULANEUM

An opportunity to explore Pompeii, one of the world's most evocative ancient sites, followed by a visit to the crater of Vesuvius, the volcano that obliterated the town. Neighbouring Herculaneum, with its manageable size and lack of crowds, is, for many, the most rewarding site of all.

DISTANCE 35km (21¾ miles) on public transport plus 11km (7 miles) on foot
TIME A full day
START Pompeii
END Herculaneum
POINTS TO NOTE
2–3 hours at Pompeii are sufficient to see the major sights, but to explore in detail you need most of the day; 2 hours is enough at Herculaneum. You will need around 3 hours for Vesuvius. Circumvesuviana trains from Naples or Sorrento run to the Pompeii Scavi – Villa dei Misteri station. Both Vesuvius and Herculaneum can be reached from Ercolano Scavi station on the same line. By car, take the A3 Naples–Salerno motorway, and exit at Pompei Ovest. To get from Pompeii to Vesuvius and Herculaneum, take the A3 towards Naples and exit at Ercolano. Sunscreen, water and sturdy shoes are essentials. A picnic is the best lunch option.

Combined Ticket
A combined ticket to Pompeii and Herculaneum costs €20, saving you €2 on the cost of separate tickets. The ticket also allows entry to the nearby archaeological sites of Boscoreale, Stabiae and the Villa Oplontis, and is valid for three days. If you buy a single ticket, you can also visit these three sites, but on the same day.

When Mount Vesuvius erupted on the afternoon of August 24, AD79, it had barely murmured for 800 years, so the widespread destruction it caused is all the more startling.

At around 1pm, Vesuvius began to spew ash and stone thousands of metres into the air. The volcanic debris rained down on the city of Pompeii, a thriving Roman town with a population of 20,000, smothering its buildings and inhabitants in a thick blanket of ash. Herculaneum, a humbler town to the west numbering fewer than 5,000 fishermen, craftsmen and farmers, and a few Roman aristocrats who had holiday homes there, was only mildly affected at this stage. As buildings in Pompeii collapsed under the avalanche of debris, only a light dusting of ash fell on Herculaneum, causing little damage but prompting most of the inhabitants to escape. Later that night, a scalding mixture of gas, ash and rock blasted Herculaneum; the town was then covered in a 20m (66ft) layer of mud.

Herculaneum was discovered by chance, in 1709, by a peasant digging a well; the first sections of Pompeii were unearthed by archaeologists of the Bourbon court of Charles III in 1748. The eruption effectively froze life in Pompeii as it was at the time, and the site has probably yielded more information about the ordinary life of Roman citizens during the imperial era than any other. Its unique importance made it an essential stop for Europeans on the Grand Tour, and has captured the imagination of visitors ever since.

POMPEII

The entrance point to the ruins of **Pompeii** ❶ (tel: 081-857 5347; www.pompeiisites.org; daily Apr–Oct 8.30am–7.30pm, last entry 6pm, Nov–Mar 8.30am–5pm, last entry 3.30pm; charge, cash only) is ancient **Porta Marina** Ⓐ. Make sure you pick up a plan of the excavations when you buy your ticket. As well as a detailed map of the site, it has timed itineraries that guide you round the most interesting sites, whether you have just a couple of hours or a whole day at your disposal.

The road leads through Porta Marina past the temples of Venus (right) and Apollo (left) and into the **Forum** Ⓑ, the centre of public life, surrounded by civic and religious institutions: temples, law courts *(basilica)*,

public offices, a wool merchants' guild and the market *(macellum)*. Straight ahead, the **Tempio di Giove** Ⓒ (Temple of Jupiter) is silhouetted against the dramatic backdrop of Vesuvius. To the left, inside the old granary stores, are displayed stacks of terracotta storage jars and plaster casts of carbonised victims. Their curled and contorted bodies evoke the full horror of the disaster.

North of the Forum

In the grid of streets north of the Forum, between the ruins of roadside tavernas and ordinary dwellings, a number of well-preserved Patrician villas reveal how the other half lived. The houses of the wealthy were walled around the outside for privacy. Light came from the open courtyards (atria) and porticoed gardens (peristyles), around which the richly decorated rooms were arranged. Two of the best examples of Roman domestic architecture are the **Casa del Fauno** Ⓓ (Via della Fortuna),

Above from far left: Teatro Grande at Pompeii; exploring the remains.

Beat the Queues In high season, the crowds at Pompeii can be overwhelming, and you can expect to queue to get into the major attractions. Get there as early as possible to avoid having to wait in line.

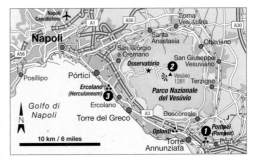

Advance Booking
Two sites at Pompeii require pre-booking (no extra fee): the Terme Suburbane and the Casa del Principe di Napoli admit a limited number of visitors every 30 minutes. Book through www.arethusa.net (tel: 081-857 5347). Also requiring pre-booking, the Casa dei Casti Amanti allows visitors to watch the restorers at work, for an additional fee (tel: 081-892 101, or www.ticketone.it).

named after the bronze statue of a dancing faun found here, and the nearby **Casa dei Vettii** (Vicolo dei Vettii), the home of rich wine merchants, its walls embellished with mythological paintings.

Villa dei Misteri

Make your way to the **Porta di Ercolano** in the northwestern corner. It's a pleasant walk along the Via dei Sepolcri, flanked with ancient funerary monuments, to the **Villa dei Misteri** **E**. This aristocratic villa outside the city walls is known for the brightly hued fresco cycle that decorates the triclinium walls, depicting the initiation ceremony of a young bride into the cult of Dionysus.

Via dell'Abbondanza

To explore the eastern end of town, head back to the Forum and the **Via dell'Abbondanza** **F**. This street lined with shops and taverns and cut through with cart tracks would have been one of the town's busiest thoroughfares. Look out for the low marble counters with circular openings. These ancient forerunners of the Italian bar served warm spiced wine from the terracotta jars under the counter. Many of the inns also had back rooms or gardens where the punters could relax and chat over a drink.

East of the Forum

On the left, the **Terme Stabiane** **G** were the city's largest baths, with

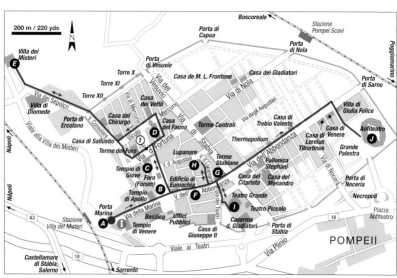

separate sections for men and women, each with its own changing rooms. The Vicolo del Lupanare leads from here to the **Lupanare** , one of 24 brothels in the city. The somewhat graphic frescoes above each doorway illustrate the resident prostitute's speciality. Opposite the baths, on the right, Via dei Teitri leads to two amphitheatres: the **Teatro Grande** ① and **Teatro Piccolo**, where plays were performed and concerts and poetry readings given; the former is still the venue for performances and events from June to September.

Anfiteatro and Palestra
At the end of Via dell'Abbondanza is the main **Anfiteatro** ②. This colossal arena could seat 15,000 spectators and was reserved for gladiatorial combat; the colonnaded **Palestra** next door was the gladiatorial training ground. If you've brought a picnic, this is the perfect place – you can sit on the high terraces and imagine Nero giving the thumbs-down from his imperial box below. Alternatively, retrace your steps to the Forum and have lunch at the **Autogrill** café, see ⑪①, located behind the Temple of Jupiter.

VESUVIUS

Take the train to the Ercolano Scavi station, which is the stop for both Vesuvius and Herculaneum. A visit to

Vesuvius ❷ (Vesuvio; access to crater: 9am–2hrs before sunset; closed in bad weather; charge), the only active volcano on the European mainland, makes a rewarding trip – all the more meaningful when paired with a visit to the towns it obliterated, AD79.

Above from far left: Pompeiian statue; a volcano victim; Dionysian mysteries are portrayed in the Villa dei Misteri.

Food and Drink

① AUTOGRILL
Pompeii Scavi; same tel and hours as Pompeii; €
Pompeii's only restaurant may be an Autogrill (also found at Italian service stations), but don't let that put you off: the food is nothing out of the ordinary, but it's freshly prepared and there's a lot to be said for an air-conditioned dining room in the heat of summer. It serves quick lunches and snacks – pizzas, pastas, salads and ice creams – and offers meal deals for €7–10.

Pompeii in Peril

Coachloads of tourists walk Pompeii's cobbled streets on a daily basis, ogling its chipped mosaics and snapping its faded frescoes. But Pompeii is now at risk for a second time: relentless foot traffic and the effects of the wind and rain on exposed ancient stones are taking their toll, and despite the site's importance, lack of investment has meant that priceless relics have been neglected for years. Though fantastically preserved for centuries by Vesuvius's volcanic ash, many of Pompeii's buildings are now in serious danger – so much so that the Italian government has declared a state of emergency in a bid to preserve what remains.

Above from far left:
wall mosaics of
Venus and Neptune;
an empty street in
Herculaneum; Karl
Briullov's *The Last
Day of Pompeii*.

Guided Treks
The Vesuvius
National Park has
nine colour-coded
trails, of varying
degrees of difficulty.
To arrange a trek
with a certified guide,
email guidevesuvio@
virgilio.it.

Climbing the Crater

Vesuvio Express services (tel: 081-
739 3666; www.vesuvioexpress.it; daily
9am–4pm; tickets from the office to
the left of the station; €10, or €16.50
including entrance to the path to the
volcano) run from Ercolano Scavi station to Vesuvius every 40 minutes. The
minibus winds its way up the fertile
slopes, planted with vineyards, to the
summit, where the landscape becomes
dark and barren, stopping 1km (½ mile)
from the top at a car park, from where
it's a 30-minute walk to the rim of the
crater. The climb is not too extreme,
but the winding lava-scree path is slip-
pery, so take care. You can peer into the
200m- (650ft-) deep crater, but you can
only go inside it on a guided walk *(see
margin)*. If the mist hasn't descended,
the view from up here is spectacular.

Meet your minibus at the allotted
time, and head back down to Ercolano
Scavi station.

HERCULANEUM

You may have reached saturation point
by now, but a visit to **Herculaneum**
❸ (Ercolano; tel: 081-732 4338;
www.pompeiisites.org; daily Apr–Oct
8.30am–7.30pm, last entry 6pm, Nov–
Mar 8.30am–5pm, last entry 3.30pm;
charge) will prove just as rewarding
as Pompeii and, because it's so much
smaller and less touristic, much less
daunting. While most of Pompeii's
buildings collapsed under the heavy
downpour of rock and ash, in Herculaneum the upper floors of many of
the houses withstood the force of the
avalanche, and the dense coating of
petrified mud encased their contents
and kept them perfectly preserved:
when excavations began, a wealth of
tools, materials, furniture, fabrics and
even plants were unearthed without
disintegrating. It's a 10-minute walk
downhill from the station, through

Vesuvius's Eruptions

Following the catastrophic eruption, AD79, the plume of
black smoke became a familiar sight on the skyline. Since
its most recent eruption in 1944, however, when the cone
collapsed into the crater, the volcano has been dormant,
though fumaroles indicate a certain amount of activity.
Today, its every movement is monitored by the Osserva-
torio Vesuviano, which has been recording data here
since 1841. You can climb to the rim safe in the knowledge that its expert vulcanologists are keeping a very
close eye on things.

Food and Drink

② **LA FORNACELLA**
90–92 Via IV Novembre, Ercolano;
tel: 081-777 4861; www.laforna-
cellasrl.it; daily 8am–midnight; €
This handily located bar-restaurant,
100m/yds from the station on the
road to Herculaneum, is ideal for a
snack or a quick meal; the two-
course set menu is good value.
They also do good pizzas – go for
the Tronchetto (topped with pro-
vola, Emmenthal and Parmesan
cheese, prosciutto and rocket).

the soulless modern town to the site; refuel at **La Fornacella**, see ⑨②, before you explore the ruins.

Cardo III

To visit the most noteworthy of Herculaneum's buildings, walk from the entrance along Cardo III to the **Casa del Tramezzo di Legno Ⓐ** (House of the Wooden Partition), so called because of the wooden screen separating the atrium from the *tablinum* (small office).

Cardo IV

On the parallel Cardo IV, the **Casa a Graticcio Ⓑ** (the Trellis House) is a humble two-storey dwelling with a balcony overhanging the street. North up the same street, the **Casa di Nettuno e Anfitrite** features a colourful mosaic of Neptune; the next-door **Casa del Bel Cortile Ⓒ** (House of the Beautiful Courtyard) holds three of the 300 skeletons unearthed by archaeologists in 1980 – a mother, father and child huddling together for comfort. At the other end of Cardo IV, seek out the **Casa dell'Atrio a Mosaico Ⓓ**, an aristocratic residence with a geometric black-and-white mosaic on the atrium floor.

Cardo V

Cardo V holds the grandest house of all, the **Casa dei Cervi Ⓔ** (House of the Deer), named after the sculptures found in the garden. Beyond here is a scenic terrace that would have overlooked the sea. South of here, the **Terme Suburbane Ⓕ** (baths) are one of Herculaneum's best-preserved sites, complete with an intact Roman door – the only one on the site not charred by fire. On the site's eastern edge, the large **Palestra** (gymnasium complex) is where public games were held.

Villa dei Papiri

Recent excavations have concentrated on the **Villa dei Papiri Ⓖ**, 150m/yds west of the exit, named after the 200 carbonised papyrus scrolls found here. Though closed at the time of writing, its many artworks and artefacts, including the Dancers of Herculaneum, can be seen in the Archaeological Museum *(see p.48)*.

Museo Archeologico Virtuale (MAV)
Near the entrance to Herculaneum at Via IV Novembre 44 (tel: 081-1980 6511; www.museomav.it; Tue–Sun 9am–5.30pm, sometimes open Mon Jan–May; charge), the sleek new MAV takes you on a virtual-reality journey through various Roman ruins, such as the Forum at Pompeii, with computer-generated reconstructions and authentic sounds and smells to ensure an all-round sensory experience.

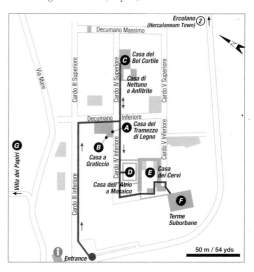

THE SORRENTINE PENINSULA

A day and a night in the lively resort town of Sorrento, followed by a leisurely drive exploring the rugged Sorrentine Peninsula that divides the Bay of Naples from the Bay of Salerno.

Sightseeing Bus
If you'd rather leave the driving to the locals, opt for the CitySightseeing Sorrento open-top bus service (tel: 081-877 4707; www.sorrento.city-sightseeing.it), which runs from outside the station in Sorrento to Massa Lubrense, Termini and Sant'Agata sui due Golfi. The round trip takes an hour and 40 minutes; you can hop on and off as the ticket is valid for 6 hours, but bear in mind that buses only run every two hours.

DISTANCE 23km (14¼ miles) on foot; 25km (15½ miles) by car
TIME Two days
START Sorrento
END Sant'Agata sui due Golfi
POINTS TO NOTE
Sorrento is easily reached from the Naples airport by Curreri coach, and from Naples by train on the Circumvesuviana line and by SITA bus from Porto Immacolatella near the port, but it's most fun to arrive by boat (from Naples' Beverello port). To explore the peninsula, you can either hire a car *(see p.95)* or a driver (www.bevenutolimos.com will tailor routes to suit you), or use the open-top CitySightseeing bus, which covers the sights in the itinerary that follows *(see margin, left)*.

The hook of land jutting from the southern end of the Bay of Naples is known as the Sorrentine Peninsula and forms part of the Monti Lattari range. Apart from Sorrento and a smattering of resort towns and hilltop villages, there is very little development, largely thanks to the inhospitable terrain in these parts. The craggy slopes are crisscrossed with ancient pathways and mule tracks that thread through olive and lemon groves into the hills and down to the sea.

SORRENTO

Travellers have been falling for the charms of **Sorrento** ❶ since ancient times: it was founded by the Greeks (the grid of streets in the old town is their legacy) and adopted by rich Romans who built luxurious villas here. It was rediscovered as a summer retreat in the 18th century, when the ongoing excavations of Pompeii made it an obligatory stop on the Grand Tour. Scores of distinguished visitors stopped off to pay a visit to the genteel resort, from Byron and Sir Walter Scott to Wagner, Henry James, Goethe and Ibsen. These days it's a lively resort town occupying a low-key middle ground between gritty Naples and the chichi resorts along the coast. Despite its lack of a decent beach, it's a good option for families, and has long been a favourite with British tourists.

Despite the crowds and tourist trappings, an air of elegance and romance prevails, and Sorrento's bustling, small-town street life makes it a rewarding place for an overnight stay.

The Harbour

The most memorable way to arrive in Sorrento is by boat from Naples. Sorrento's harbour, Marina Piccola, huddles at the bottom of the long cliff on which the town is perched. Either walk south along Via Marina Piccola, then take the long flight of steps up to town, or hop on a bus from the harbour (buy your ticket from the information kiosk beforehand) up to Piazza Tasso. Most major hotels are within walking distance, but if you have luggage there are buses and taxis on the square.

Piazza Tasso

Sorrento's compact, walkable centre can easily be explored in half a day. Start at **Piazza Tasso** Ⓐ, the town's hub, flanked by bars and cafés, and busy day and night. Head west along busy, boutique-lined **Corso Italia**, stopping at **Primavera**, see ⑪①, the cream of the town's many *gelaterias*.

The Old Town

Continue west until you reach the **Duomo** Ⓑ (tel: 081-878 2248; daily 8am–6.30pm; free). Sorrento's cathedral is unremarkable in itself, but the choir stalls show the local art of marquetry *(intarsia)* at its intricate best.

Don't miss the lovely *presepe* to the left of the entrance, in which the news of Christ's birth interrupts the locals as they sit down to a fish dinner.

Beyond the Duomo, cross the road and venture into the old town. Running parallel to Corso Italia, the skinny **Via San Cesareo** Ⓒ is a riot of souvenir shops, hawking lurid bottles of *limoncello*, the sweet and sticky local liqueur *(see margin, right)*, bright ceramics, inlaid boxes, and a whole host of lemon-themed knick-knacks. On the corner of Via Giuliani is the **Sedile Dominova** Ⓓ, a beautiful 16th-century loggia, with a domed trompe l'oeil cupola, that was the summer meeting place for Sorrentine aristocrats. Today, it is the domain of old men who sit around tables under the majolica dome playing cards and talking politics.

Villa Comunale

Walk downhill from here along Via Giuliani, turning right on to Via Vittorio Veneto, then left for the **Villa Comunale** Ⓔ (mid-Apr–mid-Oct 8am–midnight, mid-Oct–mid-Apr 8am–8pm; free), a shady park at the

Above from far left: Sorrento harbour; Duomo artwork.

Limoncello

Limoncello – the sticky, sweet local liqueur – is everywhere you look in Sorrento. Most restaurants will serve you a shot of it at the end of your meal, or you can taste it in one of the dedicated shops in town. Limoncello (Via San Cesareo 49–53; tel: 081-807 2782) also sells *limoncello* sweets and chocolates; even the local *scialatielli* pasta is lemon-scented. At I Giardini di Cataldo (Corso Italia 267; tel: 081-807 4181) you can stroll through the family's lemon grove before sampling their zesty home-made *limoncello* and ice cream.

Food and Drink 🍴

① PRIMAVERA

Corso Italia 142; tel: 081-807 3252; daily 9am–midnight; €
This always-crowded *gelateria* is plastered with photos of celebrities enjoying the excellent ice cream made here. The *agrumeto Sorrentino* and *crema di limone* flavours, made with local lemons, are delicious.

Marquetry Marvels

If the Duomo has piqued your interest in marquetry work, you can see more lovely examples of the local craft in the Museo Bottega della Tarsialignea (Via San Nicola 28; tel: 081-877 1942; www.alessandrofiorentinocollection.it; Tue–Sun 9.30am–1pm, 4–8pm, closes 7pm Nov–Mar; charge). The elaborate 18th-century inlaid wood furnishings show remarkable craftsmanship, and there are also paintings and photographs of the town in the 19th century.

cliff's edge with wonderful views over the bay. At the edge of the park stands the Baroque church of **San Francesco** **F** (tel: 081-878 1269; daily 9am–noon, 4.30–6.30pm; free) its bell tower topped with an onion dome. The medieval cloister makes a stunning venue for the classical and jazz concerts of the **Sorrento Festival** in summer; ask at the tourist office for programme details.

The Beach

From the Villa Comunale, take the steps down to the beach platforms of **Marina Piccola** **G**. Sorrento is not known for its beaches, but if your hotel doesn't have a pool, the handful of public *stabilimenti* (Apr–early Oct) are well placed for soaking up the sun. You'll pay around €15 per day for entrance and a sunlounger, and most

have a snack bar on site. Head for **Leonelli's Beach** (tel: 081-878 1644; www.leonellisbeach.com), the largest *stabilimento*, whose stripy beach huts give it an old-fashioned feel, or next-door **Marameo** (tel: 081-878 3381; www.marameobeach.com), a little pricier and sleeker, with floating sunbeds, as well as four-poster loungers for two.

Basilica di Sant'Antonino

Back at San Francesco, take the road bearing left, which opens out on to Piazza Sant'Antonino, planted with shady palms and orange trees. Overlooking the square, the **Basilica di Sant'Antonino** **H** (tel: 081-878 1437; daily 8am–6.30pm; free) has an ornate Baroque interior, from its chandeliers to its gold ceiling panels. Look out for the ex-votos from shipwrecked sailors: the

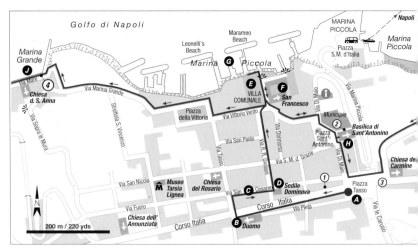

local Saint Antoninus apparently rescued a child after it had been swallowed by a whale, and as such is the protector of those at sea. Outside the church, turn sharp right to reach **Il Buco**, see ⑪②, tucked into the church's stone vaults.

Museo Correale di Terranova

Back on the piazza, turn left to rejoin Piazza Tasso, left along Corso Italia and left again at the canary-yellow church into Via Correale. A five-minute stroll takes you to the **Museo Correale di Terranova** ❶ (Via Correale 48; tel: 081-871 846; Wed–Mon 9.30am–1.30pm; charge). The museum gets its name from brothers and art connoisseurs Alfredo and Pompeo Correale, counts of Terranova, who bequeathed their family's art collection to the city in 1924. Paintings by Neapolitan greats

such as Luca Giordano and Giovanni Lanfranco, silverware, bronzes, *presepe* figurines, and a whole floor dedicated to porcelain and majolica make up the varied collection. Set in orange and lemon groves, the villa also boasts a terrace with panoramic views of the Bay of Naples.

Marina Grande

Join the post-*passeggiata* throngs for an *aperitivo* in Piazza Tasso; buzzy **Bar Fauno**, see ⑪③, is the best place to kick off your evening. From here it's a 20-minute walk down to **Marina Grande** ❶. Make your way to Piazza della Vittoria and follow Via Marina Grande down to the harbour, confusingly called Marina Grande, the 'Big Port', as opposed to Marina Piccola, or 'Little Port': it is in fact the smaller

Above from far left: splashing out; beach life; Marina Grande.

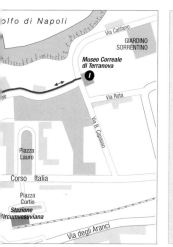

Food and Drink

② IL BUCO

Rampa Marina Piccola 5; tel: 081-878 2354; www.ilbuco ristorante.it; Thur–Tue 12.30–2.30pm, 7.30–11pm; €€€€
Don't be fooled by the name ('The Hole'): this swanky, Michelin-starred establishment is Sorrento's top restaurant, serving up dishes such as lamb in a potato crust with sweet-and-sour vegetables. Tasting menus range from €55 for three courses to €100 for an eight-course feast. Eat in the ancient brick-arched dining room or outside on stepped terraces.

③ FAUNO BAR

Piazza Tasso 4; tel: 081-878 1135; www.faunobar.it; daily 7am–2am; €
This venerable old-timer has a real buzz about it in the evening, when white-jacketed waiters weave between the tables, carrying trays of *aperitivi*. An outdoor table here is pricier than elsewhere – but worth it for the prime location.

Santa Maria all'Annunziata

After Massa Lubrense, a worthwhile detour from the tourist trail is to Santa Maria all'Annunziata, a five-minute drive away, with a stage-set piazza offering beautiful views of Capri and Ischia; the handsome Palazzo di Gioacchino Murat in the square housed Napoleon's brother-in-law. The village also has an excellent restaurant, La Torre (Piazzetta Annunziata 7; tel: 081 808 9566; daily noon–3.30pm).

and more down-at-heel of the two, but all the more charming for it. The tiny church of Sant'Anna in the harbour, with an array of ex-votos, is sometimes atmospherically candlelit at night.

The harbour is one of the most authentic corners of Sorrento – children play street football, locals chat, and the usual clutter of souvenir stalls in the old town is conspicuously absent. In the evening, the restaurants that hog the waterfront twinkle invitingly; for atmosphere, **Da Emilia**, see ①④, is hard to beat.

THE PENINSULA

Spend your second day exploring the Sorrento Peninsula. Exit Sorrento on Via Capo, which begins at the eastern end of Corso Italia. At the first fork turn right and follow the signs to Massa. The first stop is the small village of **Capo di Sorrento ❷**, where you can take the steep Roman road down towards the sea. It's a 10-minute walk past olive trees and oleander bushes to the ruins of the 1st-century **Villa di Pollio Felice**, spread across a precipice. A wooden walkway skirts the rocky coast to the Bagni della Regina Giovanna, a rocky beach with crystal-clear water.

Punta Campanella

The next settlement is **Massa Lubrense ❸**, actually 17 hamlets divided by olive groves. Make a pit stop in the square, admire the 16th-century Neapolitan paintings inside the church, and gaze at the view from the belvedere before moving on to **Termini ❹**, the departure point of one of the loveliest walks on the peninsula. Park outside the yellow church and follow the signs to the Punto Panoramico to reach **Punta Campanella ❺**. The road soon gives way to a footpath that descends slowly through terraced lemon and olive groves, past a Saracen watchtower, to the tip of the peninsula. The point is thought to be named after the warning bell *(campanella)* that was rung when Turkish pirates were sighted. The views from here are breathtaking and Capri is so close you could almost reach out and touch it. Allow for about two hours in total.

Food and Drink 🍴

④ DA EMILIA

Via Marina Grande 62; tel: 081-807 2720; daily 12.15–3pm, 7–10.30pm; €

This little waterfront trattoria has been run by the same family since 1947, and its friendly, homely atmosphere ensures that it's packed every night. It may not serve the fanciest food in the harbour – dinner may be spaghetti with clams or mussels with lemon – but it's impeccably cooked and very tasty.

⑤ DON ALFONSO 1890

Corso Sant'Agata 11–13; tel: 081-878 0026; www.don alfonso.com; Mar–mid-June, mid-Sept–Oct Wed–Sun 12.30–2.30pm, 8–10.30pm; mid-June–mid-Sept Tue–Sun 8–10.30pm, but the outside grill is open for lunch; €€€€
Superchef Alfonso Iaccarino uses produce from his farm to create the culinary masterpieces this two-Michelin-starred restaurant is renowned for. The dining room is suitably elegant – all Murano glass and hand-painted majolica – and tasting menus range from €140 to €155. Book well in advance.

Bay of Ieranto

The coast from here to Positano is wild and rugged. The limestone cliffs sliced with deep ravines plunge into hidden coves that can only be reached by boat. It's largely inaccessible by car but a walker's paradise. The villages are linked by a series of footpaths that take you through citrus groves, chestnut and oak copses, and uninhabited areas blanketed in thick Mediterranean vegetation; see www.giovis.com for routes.

Marina del Cantone is the only bay with a road link. On the winding road down to the bay is the sleepy village of **Nerano** ❻. From its piazza you can make the 45-minute walk along the cliffs to the **Marina di Ieranto** ❼, where you'll be rewarded with a spectacular beach – one of the peninsula's prime swimming spots, though very crowded on summer weekends.

Marina del Cantone

The road ends at **Marina del Cantone** ❽. It has a small, pebbly beach, but the real draw is its top-notch seafood restaurants. The **Taverna del Capitano** *(see p.105)* is one of the best places.

Sant'Agata sui due Golfi

The scenic road up to the town of **Sant'Agata sui due Golfi** ❾ is lined with olive groves, as well as myrtle, gorse and strawberry trees; even wild orchids thrive in this fertile soil. Sant'Agata is a nondescript town that has been put on the map thanks to one of Italy's

most famous restaurants – gourmets travel for miles to sample the culinary masterpieces served up at **Don Alfonso 1890**, see ⑪⑤. The church on the same square has a beautiful altar inlaid with mother-of-pearl and lapis lazuli. Follow the signs 1km (½ mile) uphill to the **Il Deserto** convent (tel: 081-878 0199; call in advance to arrange access). The building looks more like a high-security prison than a convent, but the views from the roof terrace are breathtaking. This is the only place along the coast from which you can see both the Gulf of Naples and the Gulf of Salerno, hence the name (*due golfi*: two gulfs). The road out of Sant'Agata joins the SS163; turn left to return to Sorrento or right to continue to Positano.

Above from far left: hiking at Punta Campanella; Sant'Agata sui due Golfi.

Monte Faito

In summer, visit Monte Faito for its lovely walks, cooling breezes and spectacular views. The *funivia* (cable car) is accessed from the Castellammare di Stabia stop on the Circumvesuviana line (Apr–Oct; every 20 mins). Bring a picnic, as there are no places to buy provisions beyond the funicular bars.

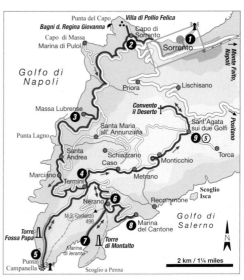

POSITANO

The coast's most photogenic town offers welcome respite from a sights-packed itinerary. It's the perfect place to spend a few hours lazing on the beach, pottering around the shops and soaking up the atmosphere.

DISTANCE 2km (1¼ miles)
TIME Half a day
START Upper town
END Fornillo Beach
POINTS TO NOTE

There is no direct transport from Naples airport to Positano or any of the Amalfi Coast towns; private transfers cost upwards of €100. Alternatively, take a Curreri bus from the airport to Sorrento (*see p.92*), and pick up one of the blue SITA buses from Sorrento station to Positano (40 minutes). In the summer months, ferries run to Positano from Sorrento and Naples, as well as from Ischia and Capri, so this tour could be combined with tours 10 and 11, although the more traditional pairing would be with the Amalfi Coast drive (*see tour 9*).

The Grotta dello Smeraldo

SITA buses run from Positano to the Grotta dello Smeraldo (Apr–Oct 9am–4pm, Nov–Mar 10am–3pm; last entry 30 mins before closing; charge). Take the lift down to sea level where eager boatmen will row you round a shadowy grotto. Inside, stalagmites and stalactites are bathed in a shimmering emerald-green light that filters through an underwater crevice in the cave wall.

With its near-vertical jumble of pastel-coloured houses clinging to cliffs that drop to a black-sand bay lined with rows of stripy parasols, **Positano** is undeniably easy on the eye. Its charms have secured its place as the coast's most chichi resort, but stroll along the beach

and you'll see that it's not entirely geared towards high-end tourism: among the serried ranks of pricey sunloungers, local families still spread out their towels en masse and tuck into picnics.

The town became fashionable after World War II. 'Positano bites deep,' wrote a spellbound John Steinbeck. 'It is a dream that isn't quite real when you are there and becomes beckoningly real after you have gone.' Positano's quiet romance disappeared with the tourists that followed in Steinbeck's wake, though something of its old magic remains, especially after dark, when the town is lit up with twinkling fairy lights and the restaurant tables spill out on to the stepped streets.

UPPER TOWN

SITA services drop off at the Sponda stop, where glorious views of the bay below make this possibly the world's most photogenic place to wait for a bus. From here, it's a short stroll along **Via Cristoforo Colombo ❶** to the lower town. If you're driving, leave your car in one of the car parks at the top end of town. Wend your way downhill, losing yourself in the whitewashed streets.

LOWER TOWN

Steeply sloping **Via dei Mulini** ❷ heads down towards the sea; stop for a pastry at **La Zagara**, see ⑪①, before exploring the town. A little further down the street, peek into the beautiful flower-filled courtyard of **Palazzo Murat** on the left, once the residence of Joachim Murat, French king of Naples in the 18th century and husband to Napoleon's sister Caroline; it's now one of Positano's loveliest hotels *(see p.99)*. Along this stretch and off the souk-like side streets are numerous little boutiques, their colourful wares spilling out into the streets.

The speciality here is clothing – mainly womenswear in light, summery fabrics, with embroidered details and floral decorations, as well as leather sandals. In the late 1950s, Positano became a fashionable shopping desti-nation; holidaying starlets stopped off to be sure their wardrobe was in vogue, and the town even inspired its own look, Moda Positano. The local stores were particularly rated for their swimwear designs, a reputation that endures.

Food and Drink

① LA ZAGARA
Via dei Mulini 8–10; tel: 089-875 964; www.lazagara.com; Easter–Oct daily 8am–1am; €
This local institution, named after the orange trees that grow on its interior terrace, has a tempting array of pastries; try the Zagara, a chocolate sponge cake made with tangerine syrup. Later on, La Zagara turns into a lively piano-bar.

② LO GUARRACINO
Via Positanesi d'America 12; tel: 089-875 794; www.lo guarracino.net; Apr–Oct daily noon–3pm, 7–11pm; €€
Comfortably distanced from the bustle of central Positano, this trattoria's scenic terrace, surrounded by olive and prickly pear trees, is what makes it special. Tasty pizzas and fish dishes are on the menu, as well as simple meat *secondi* such as veal escalope in lemon sauce. Booking is essential on summer evenings.

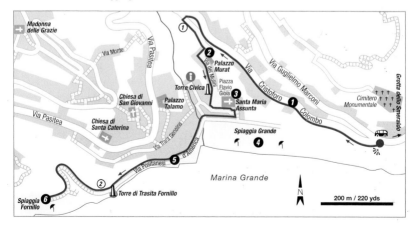

Above from far left: exploring Positano; Amalfi rooftops.

Black Madonna
According to local lore, when Saracen pirates stole the Black Madonna icon from Santa Maria Assunta, they were prevented from leaving Positano's shores by a sudden storm. When the Saracens heard a booming command from Heaven to put it back ('*posa, posa*', or 'put it down' in Latin), they set it back on the shore. The storm promptly abated and they were able to set sail again.

Santa Maria Assunta

Via dei Mulini's overhead trellis hung with pink bougainvillea makes this a stunning approach to **Santa Maria Assunta** ❸ (Piazza Flavio Gioia; tel: 089-812 2511; www.chiesapositano. com; daily 8am–noon, 4–8pm; free). The church's distinctively Moorish green-and-yellow-tiled dome graces every postcard you'll see of Positano: an exotic, glittering foil to the faded Mediterranean hues of the houses that surround it. Inside is the prized 13th-century Black Madonna icon, which is thought to hold the origins of the town's name *(see margin, left)*.

Spiaggia Grande

Take the steps from the piazza down to the **Spiaggia Grande** ❹, the town's main beach and one of Positano's major draws – although shingly, the

water is clean and the beach is broad and backed by bars and restaurants. It can be very crowded and touristic in high summer; expect to pay upwards of €15 for a day's sunlounger hire here. There is a small *spiaggia libera* ('free beach'), a sunlounger-free patch that's popular with families, but this is inevitably towel-to-towel in high season.

Via Positanesi d'America

Take **Via Positanesi d'America** ❺, the seafront path that begins by the harbour and links the town's two beaches. The path winds along the bottom of the cliff, passing the Torre Trasita, one of the coast's many watchtowers, and **Lo Guarracino**, see ⑪② *(p.67)*. The path also offers glorious views of the cluster of islets called **Li Galli**; thanks to its resemblance to a curvaceous woman floating in an azure sea, locals have nicknamed it Brigitte Bardot – appropriate for the place where Ulysses is thought to have been tempted by the seductive song of the sirens.

Spiaggia Fornillo

At the end of the path is **Spiaggia Fornillo** ❻, the beach that takes its name from the bakers' ovens in use here in Roman times. It's more down-to-earth than the Spiaggia Grande, with a few low-key beach bars and restaurants. The Fornillo district clings to the hillside behind, its peaceful white-washed lanes a world away from the glitz of central Positano.

Boat Trips

If there's one place on the Amalfi Coast that deserves to be seen from the sea, it's Positano. Several companies set up shop on the beaches in summer, offering organised day trips to Capri, along the Amalfi Coast, and to the Emerald Grotto *(see margin, p.66)*, as well as sunset cruises to the Li Galli islands (although as this is private land, you can't go ashore). Alternatively, rent your own boat from €60 per hour, or €70 per hour with skipper. Try Blue Star on the Spiaggia Grande (tel: 089-811 888; www.bluestarpositano.it) or L'Uomo e il Mare at the ferry terminal (tel: 089-811 613; www.gennaroe salvatore.it). Centro Sub Costiera Amalfitana (tel: 089-812 148; www.centrosub.it) organises diving excursions.

AMALFI AND RAVELLO

One of the world's iconic drives, the serpentine Amalfi Coast road is breathtaking and nerve-jangling in equal measure. The tour takes in two of the coast's loveliest towns, Amalfi and Ravello, and an optional hike in the beautiful Lattari mountains.

Whether you take the bus or brave it in a car, the drive along the Costiera Amalfitana is one heart-stopping journey you won't forget. The 50km (31-mile) ribbon of road snakes its way between Sant'Agata sui due Golfi and Salerno, with vertiginous views of the sea below and the mountains above.

AMALFI

Having passed Positano (see tour 8), the road winds its way round plunging valleys and soaring cliffs that drop almost sheer into the sea. The first major stop is cheerful **Amalfi** ❶. At the height of its power in the 11th century, the Maritime Republic of Amalfi rivalled the northern ports of Pisa, Genoa and Venice. Amalfitan merchants traded with Byzantium, Asia Minor and Africa, transforming their town into the most important port in southern Italy.

Nestling in a ravine, its tightly packed houses seem to tumble down to the diminutive port below. Cars and buses park outside the city wall on Piazza Flavio Gioia. Along the seafront is the tourist office, which supplies maps and information.

DISTANCE 12km (7½ miles) on foot, or 22km (13½ miles) including the Sentiero degli Dei, plus 3.5km (2 miles) by car or public transport
TIME Two days
START Amalfi
END Montepertuso
POINTS TO NOTE
The corniche coast road (SS163) requires nerves of steel – buses rocket round the bends with nonchalant ease, but only the most confident drivers should attempt the same. Traffic can be appalling in summer, so set out early. If you'd rather leave the driving to the locals, take the regular blue SITA bus service to Amalfi from Sorrento railway station (1hr 30 mins) or from Naples' Porto Immacolatella (2hrs 25 mins). Queue early for a window seat (on the right going out and the left coming back). There are frequent buses from Amalfi to Ravello (25 mins). In the summer months, boat services operate between Sorrento and the Amalfi Coast resorts.

Reaching the Coast
If the Amalfi Coast is your main destination and you're on a budget, consider breaking your journey from the airport with a night in either Sorrento or Naples, as there is no direct transport from the airport to the coast; the trip involves a number of buses and several hours, unless you opt for a shuttle service like Amalfi Coast Airport Shuttle (tel: 334-662 0218, www.amalfi coastairportshuttle. com; from €25).

Above from far left
and below right:
aspects of Amalfi's
striking Duomo.

Duomo and Town Centre

Pass through the arch into Piazza Duomo, dominated by the **Duomo** Ⓐ (daily 7.30am–7.30pm; 10am–5pm, entrance through the Chiostro, *see below*; church free, Chiostro charge), a striking example of Arab-Norman architecture. A steep flight of steps leads to the Moorish archways and facade inlaid with geometric mosaics – a 19th-century reconstruction of the medieval original. The bell tower (1276) and bronze doors, cast in Constantinople in the 11th century, are from the original structure, as is the **Chiostro del Paradiso** (1266). This

atmospheric cloister with Arabesque arches was the cemetery of Amalfitan nobles. In the crypt lies part of the skull of St Andrew, patron saint of Amalfi, to whom the Duomo was dedicated in the 9th century.

Back on Piazza Duomo, stop for a sweet treat at historic **Pansa**, see ⑪①. The square is awash with day-trippers, but off the main drag you'll soon leave the crowds behind and lose yourself in the narrow, whitewashed side streets and covered alleyways. Among the countless souvenir shops is the odd gem, such as **Antichi Sapori d'Amalfi** (Supportico Ferrari 4; tel: 089-872 062), a great place for souvenirs like fruity liqueurs in many flavours.

Maritime Festival

Every year in late May or early June, Amalfi celebrates its maritime pedigree in the Festa delle Antiche Repubbliche Marinare, with events all over town. Every four years, the regatta of the four historic maritime republics – Amalfi, Pisa, Venice and Genoa – comes to town, with a spectacular boat race ending in the harbour.

Paper Museum

Further north up the main **Via Pietro Capuano** Ⓑ, the touristic shops peter out, and once you reach Via delle Cartiere, Amalfi takes on an entirely different persona, more villagey and with the odd reminder of the industry that was once the town's big earner: 60 paper mills once operated here. The **Museo della Carta** Ⓒ (Paper Museum; Valle dei Mulini 23; tel: 089-830 4561; Mar–Oct daily 10am–6.30pm, Nov–Feb Tue–Sun 10am–3.30pm; charge), gives demonstrations in the 13th-century paper mill downstairs.

Valle dei Mulini

Opposite the museum, the road that leads round to the right, then the

steps up to the left lead to the **Valle dei Mulini** ❶ ('Valley of the Mills'), a wooded valley of wild flowers and waterfalls, which ends in a backdrop of terraced lemon groves: a walk of around an hour and a half.

ATRANI

From Amalfi's waterfront, it's a 15-minute stroll east to **Atrani** ❷, a workaday place with some good, authentic trattorias. Walk past the Saracen tower (now the restaurant of the Hotel Luna Convento, where Ibsen wrote *A Doll's House*) and around the headland to reach the beach. It has the same silvery sand as in Amalfi, but makes a much more peaceful place to laze in the sun. **Le Arcate**, see ②,

right by the beach, is a lovely spot for lunch, after which you could explore Atrani's whitewashed alleyways, dazzling in the sunshine.

RAVELLO

Back on the coast road, take the left turn to Ravello, just past Atrani. The road climbs steeply for a few kilometres until the picture-perfect town comes into view, spilling down the hillside. Between the 11th and 13th centuries, wealthy merchants imported the Moorish artefacts and architectural styles that remain one of the town's glories.

Of the three main resorts along the coast, lofty **Ravello** ❸ is the more refined and tranquil, offering good accommodation *(see p. 99)*. Alternatively,

Cookery Classes
Ravello has the best cookery school on the Amalfi Coast, Mamma Agata (Piazza San Cosma 9; tel: 089-857 019; www. mammaagata.com). A class in chef Mamma Agata's clifftop home starts with a slice of her renowned lemon cake and ends with a gourmet meal that pupils have prepared themselves. A lesson costs €190; wine appreciation courses are also available, from €150 per day.

Food and Drink 🍴

① PANSA
Piazza Duomo 40, Amalfi; tel: 089-871 065; www.pasticceria pansa.it; daily 7.30am–midnight; €
This historic *pasticceria* is an elegant spot for a coffee, lined with vintage wood cabinets and age-spotted mirrors. Be sure to try one of Pansa's citrus specialities: *delizia al limone*, stuffed with lemon cream and flavoured with *limoncello*, or chocolate-coated candied orange peel.

② LE ARCATE
Largo Cav. Orlando Buonocore, Atrani; tel: 089-871 367; www.learcate.net; Tue–Sun 12.30–3.15pm, 7.30pm–midnight, Mon also July–Aug; €€
Tucked into a corner of Atrani's harbour, Le Arcate's waterfront tables enjoy a location that can't be matched in Amalfi. The simple menu is strong on fish – grilled catch of the day with a simple salad makes a delicious lunch – and there are pizzas in the evening.

Walks from Ravello

There are several lovely country walks that start from Ravello, from the easy stroll to the nearby village of Scala, to the longer, meandering walk to Amalfi. Ask at the tourist office for a free walking map.

buses usually run back down to Amalfi quite late, so you could have dinner here before heading back down; www.ravellotime.it has up-to-date schedules, or ask at the helpful tourist office (Via Roma 18bis; tel: 089-857 096).

The Duomo

The town is closed to traffic, so park outside and walk in. The bus from Amalfi stops outside a tunnel that leads straight to the main Piazza del Duomo, the archetypal small-town Italian square, with a handful of cafés and shops arranged around a medieval cathedral. The **Duomo** (daily 8.30am–1pm, 3–8pm; free) is dedicated to St Pantaleone and holds two splendid Byzantine pulpits, one held aloft by six fierce lions, the other decorated with a mosaic of Jonah and the Whale.

Villa Rufolo and Villa Cimbrone

The real reason for coming to Ravello is its two lovely villas – or more accurately, their gardens. **Villa Rufolo ❹** (summer daily 9am–8pm; winter daily 8am–sunset; charge), in the shadow of the cathedral, was built in the Moorish style by the Rufolo dynasty, the richest family in medieval Ravello. Here, Wagner found inspiration for the magic garden in *Parsifal*, his last opera, in 1880. In summer, the luxuriant gardens host the prestigious Ravello Festival *(see box)*.

The town's other landmark is the **Villa Cimbrone** (daily 9am–30min before sunset; charge), a pleasant 15-minute walk from the square along narrow flower-filled streets. The villa was designed in the early 20th century by the eccentric Lord Grimthorpe, best known for designing the Westminster Clock. It is now a luxury hotel, but you can still visit the beautiful terraced gardens and the magnificent balcony, its balustrade lined with busts, hanging 300m (980ft) above sea level and offering stunning views.

Ravello Festival

Every year, from July to September, sleepy Ravello adjusts to a huge increase in visitor numbers as it hosts the world-renowned Ravello Festival (tel: 089-858 422; www.ravellofestival.it), a series of open-air concerts by prestigious performers. A concert under the stars in such atmospheric locations as Villas Rufolo and Cimbrone is a spine-tingling experience not to be missed by classical music fans. An added attraction is the space-age auditorium, designed by Brazilian architect Oscar Niemeyer. Ten years in the making, it is expected to be put to use as a venue for the 2011 season, offering both impressive acoustics and staggering views.

Back in Piazza del Duomo, take Via Roma on the opposite side of the square for **Cumpà Cosimo**, see ①③.

THE PATH OF THE GODS

If you have a day to spare, consider venturing out on one of the many walking trails that cut through the Monti Lattari. One of the best is the **Sentiero degli Dei ❺** – the Path of the Gods, between the mountain villages of Bomerano, west of Amalfi, and Nocelle, east of Positano. The trail is well marked, and local tourist offices have maps and information.

Catch the earliest bus you can from Amalfi to Bomerano; the trail markings begin at the main square. It's a gentle three-hour walk through vineyards, lemon and cypress groves, and wild Mediterranean *macchia* (scrub) along a path suspended between sea and sky. The views are awe-inspiring. The walk ends at Nocelle, where the sky-high **Trattoria Santa Croce**, see ①④, serves wonderful home-cooking.

MONTEPERTUSO

If the walk has left you weak at the knees, take the bus from Nocelle that winds down to Positano via **Montepertuso ❻**. Alternatively, walk along the same road – a gentle descent – then take the thousand steps down to the centre of Positano *(see tour 8)*, from where there are buses to Amalfi.

On the descent to Montepertuso, look out for the huge hole that pierces a vast rock on the mountainside. As local legend has it, the hole was created by the Virgin Mary when the Devil challenged her to a contest: whoever pierced the rock would own the land. When Mary touched the rock, it crumbled, leaving a hole that swallowed her opponent up. On 2 July, the legend is commemorated with a spectacular firework display.

Food and Drink 🍽

③ CUMPÀ COSIMO
Via Roma 44–46, Ravello; tel: 089-857 156; daily noon–3pm, 7–11pm; €€€
Family-run since its opening in 1929, this one-room trattoria may look homely but it has hosted a galaxy of celebrity diners over the years, from Jackie Onassis to Mariah Carey. The cooking is simple but delicious: you might have ham and figs to start, followed by grilled prawns, rounded off with home-made cheesecake.

④ TRATTORIA SANTA CROCE
Via Nocelle 19, Nocelle; tel: 089-811 260; daily noon–3.30pm, 7.30–10.30pm, Sat–Sun only in winter; €€
Reward yourself after the Sentiero degli Dei with lunch at this tranquil restaurant. The antipasti plate makes a generous starter to share, and the mixed grill – the house speciality – is sure to replenish a few burned calories. Book a window table to make the most of the stunning views.

Above from far left: Ravello in bloom; hiking on the Sentiero degli Dei; cheerful ceramics in Ravello.

Guided Walks
Giovanni Visetti (tel: 339-694 2911; www.giovis.com) is an experienced walking guide with a wealth of knowledge on trails all over the coast. Giovanni also runs a walking club – experienced hikers are welcome to join the walks for free. See www.freeramblers.com for details.

CAPRI

An overnight stay on one of the Mediterranean's most dazzling islands, taking in its two towns – glitzy Capri and lofty Anacapri – and walking its beautiful coastline, with panoramic views at every turn.

DISTANCE 8.5km (5¼ miles) on foot plus 7.5km (4½ miles) by public transport

TIME Two days

START The Piazzetta

END Grotta Azzurra

POINTS TO NOTE

Hydrofoils and ferries to Capri depart regularly from Naples and Sorrento. Buy your return ticket early if you're not staying the night, as the later boats fill up quickly. Most people visit Capri on a day trip, but after dark it's magical, so staying overnight is well worth considering *(see p.100)*, but book well in advance. Most hotels close from November to mid-March. Note that the Blue Grotto is closed if the sea is rough. Capri is very hilly, so for the walks you'll need sturdy footwear and a reasonable level of fitness.

Capri Transport

If you're planning to move around a lot, pick up a UnicoCapri day pass (€6.90), which covers you for unlimited bus journeys and a return journey on the funicular. Single tickets cost €1.40. Alternatively, get around on two wheels: Rent a Scooter, in Marina Grande (280 Via Provinciale; tel: 081-837 7941; daily 9am–6pm; €15 per hour or €50 per day), is right by the harbour. The island's elegant open-top taxis are plentiful, but predictably expensive.

With its soaring cliffs, emerald waters, lush vegetation and whitewashed towns, Capri is a capsule of Mediterranean beauty. The Emperor Augustus fell in love with the island when he arrived here in 29BC and traded the fertile island of Ischia for this rocky paradise that had belonged to Naples. His adopted son Tiberius ruled the Roman Empire from here until his death. Capri's charms have been exalted by playwrights, poets and novelists through the ages, but these days, it is the island's jet-set glamour that is a magnet to visitors – a reputation that is entirely deserved. Despite the hordes of day-trippers, Capri remains an essential summer stop-off for the super-rich.

AROUND CAPRI TOWN

Boats arrive at **Marina Grande**. Before catching the funicular up to **Capri Town ❶**, buy tickets at the kiosk *(see margin, left)*.

You emerge from the funicular on Piazza Umberto I. Known to all as the **Piazzetta**, this diminutive square, overlooked by the Byzantine Baroque church of **Santo Stefano**, is the departure point for many lovely walks; the best is the 45-minute stroll up to Villa Jovis, the ancient ruins of Tiberius's palace on the eastern tip of the island. Exit the square on Via Le Botteghe in the far right-hand corner and follow

the well-marked route through the whitewashed streets, past walled gardens and olive groves. The climb is steep at points, but worth the effort for the views over the Bay of Naples.

Villa Jovis and the Arco Naturale

Villa Jovis ② (daily 9am–1hr before sunset; charge) was the grandest of 12 palaces that the emperor Tiberius had built on Capri. He ruled the Roman Empire from here for 10 years, between wild orgies and nights of debauchery. On the highest point is the **Salto di Tiberio** (Tiberius's Leap), from where the emperor hurled his enemies and unsatisfactory lovers. Nowadays it's an evocatively overgrown ruin, inhabited by a docile herd of goats.

On the way back down, when you reach the crossroads at the bottom of Via Tiberio, turn left into Via Matermánia and follow signs to the **Arco Naturale ③**, a huge outcrop of limestone rock that has been eroded by the sea into a natural arch. Backtrack up the winding path to **Le Grottelle**, see 🍴① *(p.77)*.

Belvedere di Tragara

From the restaurant, steps lead down to a coastal footpath and the **Grotta di Matermánia ④**, a cave converted into a *nymphaeum* (a fountain dedicated to water nymphs) by the Ancient Romans. Further along, the strange red villa balanced on the edge of a low-lying promontory to your left belonged to the eccentric writer Curzio Malaparte (1898–1957). The path ends at the panoramic terrace of the **Belvedere di Tragara ⑤**, with captivating views of the **Faraglioni**, a trio of rocks that is the habitat of the rare blue lizard.

Above from far left: stunning panoramas abound on Capri; Villa Jovis.

Hotel Punta Tragara
With a prime location on the Belvedere di Tragara, the terracotta-coloured Hotel Punta Tragara was designed in the 1920s by Le Corbusier and was used by the Americans in World War II, hosting both Eisenhower and Winston Churchill.

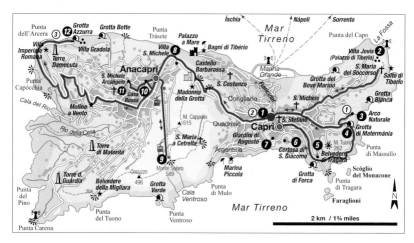

Above from left:
inside the Certosa di San Giacomo; looking down from Monte Solaro; the lush garden at Villa San Michele.

Via Krupp
Directly below the Giardini di Augusto, Via Krupp zigzigs in a series of hairpin bends to Marina Piccola (a 20-minute walk) – an unspectacular strip of beach with a few cafés and beach huts, but good enough for a swim. The road was financed in 1898 by German tycoon Friedrich Krupp to connect the Hotel Quisisana, where he lived, with the sea.

Certosa di San Giacomo

It's a short walk back into the centre along Via Tragara and Via Camerelle, where you can browse in the exclusive, white-canopied boutiques of Prada, Gucci, Ferragamo et al. At the top of Via Camerelle, turn left after the historic Hotel Quisisana into Via Serena, which leads to the **Certosa di San Giacomo ❻** (tel: 081-837 6218; Tue–Sat 10am–1pm; charge). This charming medieval charterhouse is now home to a small museum, containing statues found in the Blue Grotto and paintings by the German Symbolist painter Karl Wilhelm Diefenbach.

Giardini di Augusto

Come out of the monastery and take the left-hand Via Matteotti at the junction with Via Serena for the **Giardini di Augusto ❼** (daily 9am–7pm), which are terraced gardens offering more dazzling views.

At sunset, the Piazzetta regains its composure. Emptied of day-trippers, the little square turns into an outdoor salon as the *beau monde* emerges from the hotels for a night out. Join them for a cocktail; Piccolo Bar is the oldest and least showy of the quartet of bars. For dinner, the terrace at **Pulalli**, see ⑪②, can't be beaten.

AROUND ANACAPRI

Day two is spent exploring Anacapri and the west coast. Capri's second town is more rustic than its worldly rival, with a Moorish influence visible in its cubic whitewashed houses. Buses from Via Roma in Capri town run to **Piazza Vittoria**, which is crammed with a riot of tacky souvenir shops.

In the piazza, walk up the steps and turn left for **Villa San Michele ❽** (34 Viale Axel Munthe; tel: 081-837 1401; www.villasanmichele.eu; Mar 9am–4.30pm; Apr and Oct 9am–5pm; May–Sept 9am–6pm; Nov–Feb 9am–3.30pm; charge), built by the Swedish doctor Axel Munthe (1857–1949) on the ruins of one of Tiberius's villas. His book, *The Story of San Michele*, describing the building of his villa was an international bestseller. The house is now a museum with a display of ancient finds and eclectic furnishings, but the lushl garden is the highlight, with its colonnaded, vine-swathed pergola framing jaw-dropping views. It makes a spectacular venue for concerts under

Sentiero dei Fortini

If you want to avoid the crowds, catch a bus from Anacapri to Punta Carena (take a bus signed 'Faro' from Via de Tommaso), one of the wildest corners of the island and the departure point for a stunning walk. The **Sentiero dei Fortini** hugs the west coast from the lighthouse at Punta Carena to the Punta dell'Arcera near the Blue Grotto, passing three ruined fortresses along the way. Mostly easy going, it takes about three hours each way. There are plenty of places for a swim en route, but returning ashore is not always easy, except at Punta Carena.

the stars in the summer. Don't miss the Egyptian Sphinx on the parapet of the chapel, on the garden's top level.

Monte Solaro

In the corner of Piazza Vittoria, a chair-lift whisks you up to the summit of **Monte Solaro** ❾ (589m/1,932ft; Apr–Oct 9.30–4.30pm; Nov–Mar 9am–3.30pm; charge). The wonderful, peaceful ride over gardens, woods and vineyards takes just under quarter of an hour, and more spellbinding views and a bar welcome you at the top.

Church of San Michele

Leading off Piazza Vittoria, Via Orlandi takes you to the Pompeiian-red **Casa Rossa** ❿ at no. 78 (tel: 081-838 2193; mid-May–mid-Sept Tue–Sun 10.30am–1.30pm, 5.30–9pm; mid-Sept–mid-May Tue–Sun 10.30am–5pm; charge), containing finds from the Blue Grotto. Continue on Via Orlandi, turning right on to Piazza San Nicola for the **Church of San Michele** ⓫ (daily 9am–7pm; charge), renowned for its vivid majolica floor depicting the expulsion from Paradise, with Adam and Eve frolicking with unicorns, peacocks and elephants.

Grotta Azzurra

If you didn't succumb to one of the boat trips offered at Marina Grande, catch a bus to the **Grotta Azzurra** ⓬ (Blue Grotto; take the right turn opposite the Casa Rossa, which emerges opposite the bus station on Via de Tommaso; 9am–3pm; charge), Capri's biggest tourist attraction. Descend the steps to the cave entrance and join the queue for the boatmen who row endless streams of tourists around the marine cavern to admire the incredible glowing light within. The best time to visit is between 11am and 1pm, when the cave walls are bathed in an intense aquamarine light, while the sandy bottom glows with silvery shadows. The restaurant **Il Riccio**, see ⑪③, is just steps from the grotto.

A Cheap Eat

Eating out in Capri can eat into your budget. Da Brioches, an excellent *alimentari* at 5 Via Fuorlovado in Capri Town (Mon–Sat 8am–9pm, Sun 9.30am–8pm), will make you up a panino for a few euros, and sells plenty of tasty treats for a picnic.

Food and Drink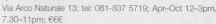

① LE GROTTELLE

Via Arco Naturale 13; tel: 081-837 5719; Apr–Oct 12–3pm, 7.30–11pm; €€€
Suspended above a verdant hillside overlooking the sea, this is an irresistible lunch spot. The food is delicious and unfussy, strong on fish dishes such as baked anchovies with local herbs. Booking is essential for a table on the panoramic terrace.

② PULALLI

Piazza Umberto 4; tel: 081-837 4108; Wed–Mon noon–3pm, 7pm–midnight, Aug open daily; €€€
Wonderfully sited in the bell tower overlooking the Piazzetta, this elegant restaurant and wine bar is reasonably priced (for Capri). *Scialatielli verdi* (pasta with prawns and rocket) is the house speciality, and the walls are lined with over 300 wines. Book to be sure of a table on the terrace.

③ IL RICCIO

Via Gradola 4–6; tel: 081-837 1380; Thur–Sat 12.30–3.30pm, 8–10.30pm, Sun–Wed 12.30–3.30pm; €€€
This waterside restaurant, in the swanky Capri Palace Hotel, has a breezy nautical decor and a classy menu. Freshly caught fish is the order of the day, from an excellent seafood buffet. There's also an on-site beach club, with secluded sun decks nestling among the rocks.

ISCHIA

This two-day tour of the lush 'emerald island' of Ischia does a loop of the island, taking in its bustling towns and stopping for a spot of pampering in its celebrated hot springs.

Vehicle Hire
Ischia is a very easy place to navigate. The best way to explore the island is by car, although hiring a scooter can be fun too. Balestrieri Rent A Car (Via Iasolino 33, tel: 081-985 691; www.autonoleggio balestrieri.it; Mon–Fri 8am–1.30pm, 3.30–7.30pm, Sat 8am–7.30pm, Sun 9am–7.30pm), behind the port to the right, charges from €30 per day for a car, €20 for a scooter.

DISTANCE 10km (6¼ miles) on foot plus 38km (23½ miles) by car or public transport
TIME Two days
START Ischia Porto
END Ischia Ponte
POINTS TO NOTE
Hydrofoils and ferries depart from Naples, Sorrento and Pozzuoli to Ischia Porto, Casamicciola and Forio. The CS bus from Ischia Porto covers the circular route described below around every 20 minutes; the loop takes around two hours. The CR follows the same route in the opposite direction; single tickets cost €1.30, day passes €4.20. Most hotels close from mid-October to Easter; published rates include half-board, but many will agree to bed and breakfast.

Ischia may not have the same rugged beauty as its neighbour, but it has great beaches and protected inland areas that are a haven for walkers. As well as yielding excellent wine, the volcanic terrain produces bubbling hot springs, prized for their therapeutic powers.

Ischia was first settled by Greek traders in the 8th century BC, followed by the Romans who flocked to its spas. But less than a century after Pompeii, Monte Epomeo erupted, destroying all life on the island. From the Middle Ages, the islanders lived in fear of marauding Saracens, who remained a threat for centuries. It wasn't until the 19th century and the advent of the Grand Tourists that Ischia regained its status as a prestigious spa resort.

AROUND ISCHIA PORTO

Most boats from Naples arrive at **Ischia Porto ❶**, a harbour whose natural boundaries once enclosed a volcanic crater lake. A string of animated fish-restaurants line the harbour.

This itinerary follows the SS270 ring road in a westerly direction. **Casamicciola Terme ❷**, the first major town, has numerous spa hotels, but the best places are elsewhere.

LACCO AMENO

Carry on to the more appealing **Lacco Ameno ❸**, site of the first Greek settlement. Just before the town beach,

the SS270 veers inland, but carry straight along the seafront to admire the town's symbol, **Il Fungo**: a rock sculpted by erosion into a distinctive mushroom shape rising out of the sea. The road ends in a little square with a bubblegum-pink church dedicated to the island's patron saint, **Santa Restituta**. The **Area Archeologica** next door (Easter–Nov Mon–Sat 9.30am–12.30pm, 5–7pm; charge) holds a wealth of Greco-Roman remains.

Just off the square, a slope climbs to the 18th-century Villa Arbusto, home to the **Museo Archeologico di Pithecusae** (Corso Rizzoli 210; tel: 081-333 0288; www.pithecusae. it; Tue–Sun 9.30am–1pm, 3–7pm; charge) and more ancient treasures.

The star exhibit is the 7th-century 'Nestor's Cup', described in the *Iliad* and bearing one of the oldest Greek inscriptions in existence, praising the wines of Ischia. The gardens are used for concerts in July and August.

NEGOMBO

The SS270 continues uphill, skirting **Monte Vico** (116m/381ft). This lofty promontory boasts the island's prettiest beach, the **Baia di San Montano**, and swankiest spa, **Negombo ❹** (Via San Montano 14; tel: 081-986 390; www. negombo.it), where 15 pools, caves and baths are arranged in terraces dotted with contemporary sculptures and immersed in lush, jungly vegetation.

Above from far left: admiring the views over Ischia; boats at Ischia Porto.

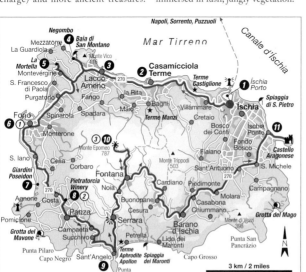

Above: befriending a local; grapes thrive in Ischia's climate.

Above from far left:
charming Forio;
Il Fungo is a symbol
of Lacco Ameno;
Castello Aragonese.

Budget Pampering
If your budget won't
stretch to a spa, head
to the little bay of
Sorgeto, near Forio,
accessible by sea or
down a long flight of
steps, where hot
mineral springs and
fumeroles bubble up
under the sea, even in
the depths of winter.
It's also worth knowing
that you can get into
the Giardini Poseidon
an hour before closing
for just €5 (the day
rate is €30).

LA MORTELLA

Hidden among the signs at the next right-hand turning is one to **La Mortella** ❺ (Via F. Calise 39; tel: 081-986 220; www.lamortella.org; Easter–Nov Tue, Thur, Sat–Sun 9am–7pm; for tours tel: 081-990 118, www.platypustour.it; charge), the estate of English composer Sir William Walton (1902–1983). It is famous for its gardens, planted with 1,200 species and lovingly cultivated over 50 years by Walton's widow, Lady Susana, until her death in 2010. Concerts and Greek theatre performances are held at weekends.

AROUND FORIO

Past La Mortella, the road carries on to the Spiaggia San Francesco, a little stretch of beach, then rejoins the SS270

at lively **Forio** ❻. Stroll into the historic centre along Corso Umberto and follow signs to the white church of **Madonna del Soccorso**, filled with votive offerings for the protection of fishermen and sailors. It shares its headland perch with the double-Michelin-starred **Umberto a Mare**, see ⑪①.

The nearest decent beach is **Citara**, most of which has been colonised by the **Giardini Poseidon** ❼ (tel: 081-908 7111; www.giardiniposeidon. it). This spa has a more old-fashioned feel than Negombo, but its 21 pools and huge range of treatments make it one of the most popular.

To sample one of the celebrated local wines, stop by the **Pietratorcia Winery** ❽ (Via Provinciale Panza 267; tel: 081-907 232; www.pietratorcia.it; Apr–mid-June, mid-Sept–mid-Nov daily 10am–1pm, 4–8pm, Fri–Sun until midnight; mid-June–mid-Sept 5pm–midnight), a prestigious wine estate that also serves delicious meals, see ⑪②.

SANT'ANGELO

Come off the SS270 at Panza and follow signs to **Sant'Angelo** ❾ on the southernmost tip of the island; park outside the town. Sant'Angelo is not the untouched fishing village it once was, but something of its old character remains in the narrow streets and stack of pastel and white houses.

East of the village is the **Terme Aphrodite Apollon** spa (tel: 081-999

Taking the Waters

According to legend, an exhausted Ulysses regained his strength after wallowing in Casamicciola's hot springs, and Ischia's 103 springs and 67 fumaroles still do an excellent job of soothing weary limbs. In high season, Italian and German spa devotees flock here to be massaged, pummelled and doused in mineral-rich waters, used to cure all ills, from arthritis to premature ageing. But if all you want is some five-star pampering, you won't be disappointed: head for Negombo for cutting-edge treatments; Giardini Poseidon and Aphrodite Apollon for good old-fashioned mud baths; and the spa at the Albergo della Regina Isabella (see p.101) for a more intimate spa experience.

219; www.hotelmiramare.it); beyond is the **Spiaggia dei Maronti**, a long stretch of public beach that can be reached via a clifftop footpath or by water taxi from the port.

MONTE EPOMEO

Back inland, the road winds its way up into the green and mountainous heartland. At the village of Fontana, take the first left after the little square, signposted for **Monte Epomeo ⑩**, which will take you halfway up the extinct volcano of Monte Epomeo, Ischia's highest point at 787m (2,582ft). Park at the bar and make the 40-minute trek to the top. Magnificent, 360° views of the whole island await you. Reward yourself with a drink at **La Grotta da Fiore**, see ⑪③.

ISCHIA PONTE

The SS270 completes its circle at **Ischia Ponte ⑪**, where the hulking **Castello Aragonese** (tel: 081-991 959; daily 9am–1hr before sunset; charge) lords it over the town. Park by the sea, then cross the lovely Ponte Aragonese to the medieval castle.

The Greeks built the first fortress on this rocky islet in 474BC. It was enlarged by subsequent rulers and, in 1441, Alfonso of Aragon strengthened the defences and added the bridge, enabling locals to take refuge within its walls during pirate attacks. By the 18th century, the island had 13 churches and a thriving community, but in 1809, under French rule, it was bombarded by the British and all but destroyed. On July 26 each year, the Festa di Sant'Anna sees a spectacular sea-borne procession staging the 'burning of the Castello Aragonese', culminating in an extravagant firework display.

Take the lift to the top, where you can wander a network of paths that take you past the ruined shells of churches, taking in the heart-stopping views from the ancient defences. If you want to wake up to that same view, book a room at Il Monastero *(see p.101)*.

Grisly History
The Castello Aragonese takes a macabre turn with its displays of instruments of torture and in the eerie cell of the Cimitero delle Monache Clarisse, in which the bodies of dead nuns were left to putrefy on stone seats for the living nuns to visit every day, as a reminder of their mortality.

Food and Drink

① UMBERTO A MARE
Via Soccorso 2, Forio; tel: 081-997 171; www.umbertoamare. it; daily noon–3pm, 7–11.30pm, closed Mon Oct–Apr; €€€€
This upscale restaurant offers panoramic views and superb but pricey fish dishes. At lunch, though, you can feast on dishes such as linguine with tuna, capers and olives for €9. There's also an elegant café (daily 9am–5pm).

② PIETRATORCIA WINERY
Via Provinciale Panza 267; tel: 081-907232; www. pietratorcia.it; for hours, see left; €€€
Dine in a beautiful rustic setting at this renowned winery. You can have a snack – €15 for a cheese and cold meat plate, plus three wines – or a full meal of local specialities, including pancakes, artisan cheeses and Ischian rabbit.

③ LA GROTTA DA FIORE
Monte Epomeo; tel: 081-999 521; www.epomeolagrotta. com; daily 9.30am–6pm; €€
The views are breathtaking from the terrace of this down-to-earth trattoria – the perfect place to rest your limbs after the climb up Monte Epomeo. They serve up rustic local specialities such as *bucatini* pasta with Ischian rabbit, and will ply you with *limoncello* until it's time to head back down.

PROCIDA

The low-key sights of the bay's smallest island can be seen in a morning,
followed by a lazy lunch in a picturesque marina, and an afternoon spent
lounging on one of the unspoilt beaches

DISTANCE 6km (3¾ miles)
TIME A leisurely day
START Marina Grande
END Lido
POINTS TO NOTE

Procida is a 40-minute hydrofoil
ride from Naples (departing from
Beverello or Mergellina) and 10
minutes from Ischia. The ferry
(from Calata Porto di Massa) takes
an hour, but you can enjoy views
of the coast from the deck.

Deep Blue Sea
Procida's limpid
blue waters are
perfect for diving.
Procida Diving Centre
(tel: 081-896 8385 or
338-722 7484; www.
vacanzeaprocida.it)
organises dives from
€70, with instructor
and equipment.

At just 4 sq km (2½ sq miles), **Procida**
is the smallest of the islands, and the
least touristic: fishing and farming are
still integral to its economy and the volcanic soil is ideal for the cultivation of
vineyards and citrus groves. But tourism
still plays an important role: in summer,
the island's population is doubled.

MARINA GRANDE

Ferries and hydrofoils dock at **Marina
Grande ❶**, a colourful jumble of boats
and sun-baked houses. The hill is dominated by the grim Castello d'Avalos,
a prison until 1988. Turn left and
meander along the harbour until you
reach the church of **Santa Maria della
Pietà** (1760) ❷. Stop for a coffee at the
Bar dal Cavaliere opposite, see ⑪①,
before taking Via Vittorio Emanuele
uphill. Bear left at the yellow church
to reach panoramic **Piazza dei Martiri**
and the yellow church of Santa Maria
delle Grazie (1679).

It's a steep 500m climb from here to
the crumbling **Abbazia San Michele
Arcangelo ❸** (winter: Tue–Sat
10am–1pm, 5–7pm, Sun 10am–1pm,
summer: Tue–Sat 10am–1pm, 3–8pm,
Sun 10am–1pm; church: free, museum:

charge), which features a coffered ceiling decorated with fine gold, and a central painting of the Archangel Michael by Luca Giordano (1699); there's also a museum with an 18th-century *presepe* and a set of catacombs. During Good Friday's atmospheric Processione dei Misteri, a life-sized wooden sculpture of Christ is carried by fishermen from the Abbazia to Marina Grande.

The whitewashed domes of the abbey church rise above the **Terra Murata**, the ruins of a once-impregnable citadel, built to defend the island from Saracen attack. On your way back down to the Piazza dei Martiri, stop at the terrace of the abandoned Castello and admire views of the ruined citadel above and Corricella below.

CORRICELLA

The enchanting fishing village of **Corricella ❹**, a warren of pastel-painted houses interconnected by arches, can be reached via the sloping road by the church. Take the steps to the left of the pink house for the harbour, where fishermen mend nets and the day's catch is served up in bijoux fish restaurants.

Another set of steps at the far end of Corricella takes you back up to the main road. Turn left into **Via Scotti**, whose high-walled gardens offer tantalising glimpses of citrus trees. Continue along Corso Vittorio Emanuele, turning left off **Piazza Olmo** on to the quieter Via Pizzaco, which commands glorious

views across the bay to the abbey and Corricella. A little way along on your left, a flight of steps leads down to the lovely **Chiaia ❺** beach, ideal for young children, and the family-run **La Conchiglia** restaurant *(see p.107).*

CHIAIOLELLA

Continue along Via Pizzaco, veering right into **Via de Gasperi**, and continue hugging the coast, enjoying views of Capo Miseno on the mainland, until you reach Via Solchiaro. Turn left then right into Via Simone Schiano, which leads to **Marina Chiaiolella ❻**, once the crater of a volcano and now a charming scene of bobbing yachts and bustling fish restaurants; stop for lunch at **Crescenzo**, see ⑪②.

On the western side of the marina is the **Lido ❼**, Procida's longest and most popular beach. Buses L1 or L2 run from Chiaiolella back to the port.

Above: Marina Grande has a cheerful appeal.

Isola di Vivara

At the southern tip of Chiaiolella beach you can see the Isola di Vivara, a tiny volcanic island joined to Procida by a footbridge. Once a hunting ground for the Bourbon kings, Vivara is now a nature reserve and bird sanctuary (closed at the time of writing). Unlike the birds, the wild rabbits that bound through the Mediterranean *macchia* (scrub) are not protected – rabbit stew is a Procidan speciality.

Food and Drink 🍴

① BAR DAL CAVALIERE

Via Roma 42; tel: 081-810 1074; Tue–Thur, Sun 7am–midnight, Fri–Sat 7am–4am; €

This bustling *pasticceria* is a good place for a coffee and a sweet treat – try the *lingua di bue*, a 'tongue' of flaky pastry, lemon-scented or stuffed with nutty chocolate.

② CRESCENZO

Via Marina Chiaiolella 33; tel: 081-896 7255; www.hotel crescenzo.it; €€

Right on the harbourfront, this restaurant serves the freshest of fish, straight off the boat. The zesty lemon tart makes a sweet finish to the meal.

DIRECTORY

A user-friendly alphabetical listing of practical information,
plus hand-picked hotels and restaurants, clearly organised by
area, to suit all budgets and tastes.

A

AGE RESTRICTIONS

The age of consent in Italy is 14. In order to drive legally in Italy you must have your full UK licence and be at least 18 years of age. There is no minimum drinking age, but you have to be over 16 to be served drinks in a public place.

B

BUDGETING

Naples is inexpensive, though prices soar in resorts along the Amalfi Coast and on Capri. A glass of house wine in Naples will cost €1.50, on Capri €4; a beer is €3 in Naples, €5 in Capri. At an inexpensive trattoria, main courses go for €5–8; in moderate places, €10–15; in expensive restaurants €18–25. Hotel rates vary hugely, but a double room in a cheap hotel in Naples will cost €50–90; a moderate hotel €90–150; in low season, de-luxe rooms are as little as €150, though in high season the sky's the limit: the fanciest places on the Amalfi Coast and islands will set you back upwards of €600. Public transport is cheap: a 90-minute ticket within Naples is €1.10, or a day return from Naples to Sorrento just €6.70. Hydrofoils are pricier: around €16 one-way from Naples to Capri, though slower ferries and the Metrò del Mare summer services (see p.94) are a little cheaper.

The major museums and archaeological sites charge from €4 to €11. Most state-run museums and sites offer free entrance to EU citizens under 18 or over 65, with a lesser discount to those aged between 18 and 25. Entrance to all churches is free. For the Campania Artecard tourist pass, see p.11.

C

CHILDREN

The family-orientated Neapolitans adore children, and little ones are fussed over in even the smartest of restaurants. The Villa Comunale has plenty of space for kids to let off steam, as well as an aquarium, and the Parco di Capodimonte is a good place to kick a ball around. Older children might enjoy a visit to Pompeii or Herculaneum – especially if it's preceded by a virtual-reality reconstruction – or the intriguing underground sights of Napoli Sotterranea and the catacombs, or the geological wonders of Vesuvius and the Solfatara. Hiring a boat in Sorrento, the Amalfi Coast or the islands and pottering between beaches can be a fun way to spend a day. If all else fails, take the kids to the Edenlandia theme park (see margin, p.23).

CRIME AND SAFETY

Despite its reputation as a hotbed of crime, Naples is no more dangerous

Above from far left: family fun on a moped; a leafy shrine; enjoying the evening sunshine.

than any other big European city, if you take the usual precautions. The main problem tourists experience is pickpocketing and bag-snatching, together with theft from parked cars. Wear bags across the body if possible and be wary of nimble-fingered lads whizzing by on mopeds. Be especially vigilant on crowded buses and around Piazza Garibaldi, the Quartieri Spagnoli and La Sanità.

Report a theft *(furto)* as soon as possible; you will need to go to the police to make a statement *(denuncia)*. The police report will be required for any insurance claim and to replace stolen documents. For information on the nearest police station, call Naples' Questura Centrale, near Piazza Municipio at Via Medina 5, tel: 081-794 1111, or ask for the *questura più vicino*.

CUSTOMS

Visitors from EU countries are not obliged to declare goods imported into or exported from Italy if they are for personal use, up to the following limits: 800 cigarettes, 200 cigars or 1kg of tobacco; 10 litres of spirits (over 22 percent alcohol) or 20 litres of fortified wine (under 22 percent alcohol).

For US citizens, the duty-free allowance is 200 cigarettes, 50 cigars; 1 litre of spirits or 2 litres of wine; one 50g bottle of perfume and duty-free gifts to the value of US$200–800, depending on how often you travel.

D

DISABLED TRAVELLERS

Central Naples is not an easy place for people with disabilities. However, things are improving, with ramps and lifts being installed in museums, stations and hotels. Capri's hotels in particular are good at meeting individual needs, and as there are no steps, it can be easier to get around, though the slopes are steep and buses are not wheelchair-accessible. The new 'Friendly Pompei' scheme makes navigation of the site easier, with a two-hour route around the site for those with reduced mobility. Call 081-772 2222 for assistance on trains, and 848 888 777 for help at the airport. The website www.accessibleitaly.com is useful for pre-trip planning, and www.turismoaccessibile.it is another excellent resource, with detailed information on accessible museums, restaurants and hotels, as well as a rundown of wheelchair-friendly trains, ferries and buses.

E

ELECTRICITY

Standard is 220 volts. Sockets are generally two round pins. For UK visitors, adaptors can be bought before you leave home, or at airports and stations. Travellers from the US will need a transformer.

LUCAN LIBRARY TEL. 6216___

EMBASSIES AND CONSULATES

If your passport is lost or stolen, you will need to obtain a police report *(see Crime and Safety, p.86)* and have proof of your identity to get a new one. Many countries have embassies in Rome, but several have consulates in Naples.

Australia: 5 Via Antonio Bosio, Rome; tel: 06-852 721; www.italy. embassy.gov.au

Canada: 29 Via Carducci, Naples; tel: 081-40 1338; www.canada.it

Ireland: 3 Piazza Campitelli, Rome; tel: 06-697 9121; www.ambasciata-irlanda.it

New Zealand: 44 Via Clitunno, Rome; tel: 06-853 7501; www.nzembassy.com

UK: 40 Via dei Mille, Naples; tel: 081-423 8911; www.britain.it

US: Piazza della Repubblica; tel: 081-5838 111; www.usembassy.it

EMERGENCY NUMBERS

National emergency number, including police and medical emergencies: 113; Carabinieri: 112; Fire: 115; Ambulance: 118.

G

GAY/LESBIAN ISSUES

Attitudes towards gay relationships in Naples and the main resorts are reasonably tolerant, though smaller towns may be more conservative. The national organisation Arcigay has a branch at Vico San Geronimo alle Monache 19, off Via Benedetto Croce; tel: 081-5528 815; www.arcigaynapoli.org. It offers information and advice, and organises events for the local gay community.

For general information on the scene in Italy, see www.gay.it.

H

HEALTH

In theory, EU and Australian citizens are entitled to reciprocal care (visitors will need to obtain an EHIC card, www.ehic.org.uk, before they go; Australians are covered by Medicare). Nonetheless, it's a good idea to take out travel insurance. The standard of care is generally high, though the state of hospitals themselves may not inspire confidence.

US citizens are not covered under Italian law, so will need to take out private health insurance.

Chemists

Chemists *(farmacie)* have a large green cross on the outside. The pharmacy at Napoli Centrale station is open 24 hours a day; *Il Mattino* newspaper carries details of late-night pharmacies.

Emergencies

If you need emergency treatment, call 118 for an ambulance or information

on the nearest hospital with an emergency department *(pronto soccorso)*.

Hospitals

Naples' most central hospitals with *pronto soccorso* (emergency) departments are in Vomero: Cardarelli at 9 Via Cardarelli; tel: 081-546 4440 and Santobono (for children under 12) at 6 Via Mario Fiore; tel: 081-220 5438.

HOURS AND HOLIDAYS

In general, shops open Mon–Sat 9am–1pm and 4–7pm or 8pm, though many close on Monday morning and Saturday afternoon. Most restaurants close on Sundays. Many shops and restaurants close for at least two weeks in August. Banks open Mon–Fri 8.30am–1.30pm and 2.45–4pm.

Opening times of churches and museums vary enormously and change twice a year, with a longer timetable for summer (Easter–Oct) and a shorter one for winter (Nov–Easter). Most churches open early in the morning but close at around noon or 12.30pm until 3pm or 4pm, closing again in the evening between 7pm and 8pm; some open in the morning only. Many museums are closed on Monday and ticket offices close one hour before the official closing time.

Archaeological sites close one hour before sunset; two hours in the case of Pompeii and Herculaneum. The times given in this guide are as accurate as possible, but may be subject to change. If in doubt, check with the tourist office *(see p.91)*.

Most businesses are closed on the following public holidays:
New Year's Day (1 January)
Epiphany (6 January)
Easter Monday
Liberation Day (25 April)
Labour Day (1 May)
Founding of the Republic (2 June)
Assumption of the Virgin Mary (15 August)
Feast of San Gennaro (Naples only, 19 September)
All Saints' Day (1 November)
Immaculate Conception (8 December)
Christmas and St Stephen's Day (25–26 December)

INTERNET FACILITIES

There is no shortage of internet cafés in Naples, especially around the station. You can expect to pay around €2–4 for an hour's internet access. Most hotels offer some form of access, from Wi-fi to a communal computer terminal. Lemme Lemme Internet bar (74 Piazza Bellini; tel: 081-295 237; Mon–Sat 9am–3am, Sun 5pm–3am; €2.50/hour) and Navig@ndo (28 Via Sant'Anna dei Lombardi; tel: 081-1936 0030; Sun–Fri 9.30am–8pm, Sat 9.30am–1.30pm; €1/30min) are both central.

Above from far left: a romantic moment in Naples; a busy beach in Báia.

M

MONEY

The unit of currency in Italy is the euro (€), which is divided into 100 cents. There are 5, 10, 20, 50, 100, 200 and 500 euro notes, coins worth €1 and €2, and 1, 2, 5, 10, 20 and 50 cent coins.

Major credit cards are accepted by most hotels, shops and restaurants, though some smaller places remain cash-only. Cash machines (ATMs), called Bancomat, can be found throughout central Naples and the main resorts, and are the easiest and generally the cheapest way of obtaining cash; in smaller towns ATMs are scarcer.

You need your passport or identification card when changing money. Not all banks will provide cash against a credit card, and some may refuse to cash traveller's cheques in certain currencies. On the whole, exchange bureaux *(cambio)* outside of touristic areas offer better rates than banks. Traveller's cheques are the safest way to carry money around, but not the most economical since banks charge a large commission for cashing them.

Service is not included in a restaurant bill unless noted on the menu as *servizio*. It is customary to leave a modest tip, but nothing like the 10–15 percent common in other countries; leaving €1–5 is the norm. When you take a taxi, just round the fare up to the nearest euro.

P

POST

Post offices are open Mon–Fri 8am–1.30pm, Sat 8am–12.30pm; the main post office in Naples is at 2 Piazza Matteotti (Mon–Fri 8am–6.30pm, Sat 8am–12.30pm). Stamps *(francobolli)* can be bought at many tobacconists *(tabacchi)* – look for the sign with the white letter 'T' on a black background. Italian postboxes are usually red with two slots, *per la città* (for the city) and *tutte le altre destinazioni* (everywhere else). For fast delivery (up to three days in Europe and five to the rest of the world), ask for *posta prioritaria* stamps.

S

SMOKING

Smoking is banned in all public spaces in Italy, except in those establishments that have created a specially ventilated smoking area, though this is rare.

T

TELEPHONES

The prefix for Italy is +39. The local code is 081.

When calling abroad from Italy, first dial 00 (the international access code), then the country code (44 for the UK; 353 for the Republic of Ireland; 1 for

Above from far left: market fish stall; enjoying a drink at the Borgo Marinaro; a giddying view on the Amalfi Coast.

the US and Canada; 61 for Australia; 64 for New Zealand), the area code and then the subscriber number. For international directory enquiries, tel: 176; for reversed-charge (collect) calls, tel: 170.

Most public payphones accept phone cards *(scheda telefonica)* only. You can buy cards in various denominations from *tabacchi* and many news-stands. Some payphones accept credit cards, and some bars have coin-operated payphones. There are a number of cheap international phone cards available from news-stands, and call centres where you can make your call and pay later.

Mobile (cell) phone reception is based on GSM technology, which is not compatible with US non-tri-band phones. If you have an unlockable GSM, dual- or tri-band phone, consider buying an Italian SIM card from local providers TIM, Vodafone or Wind, which cost from €10. Numbers starting with a 3 are mobile numbers and will cost more to call.

TIME ZONES

Italy follows Central European Time (GMT+1). From the last Sunday in March to the last Sunday in September, clocks are advanced one hour (GMT+2).

TOURIST INFORMATION

Naples: 7 Piazza del Gesù, tel: 081-551 2701; 9 Via San Carlo, tel: 081-402 394; 107 Via Santa Lucia, tel: 081-245 7475; there's also a branch at the airport. The tourist board's website, www.inaples.it, is useful.

Campi Flegrei: 3 Via Campi Flegrei, Pozzuoli, tel: 081-526 6639.

Pompeii: 1 Via Sacra, tel: 081-850 7255.

Sorrento: 35 Via L. De Maio, tel: 081-807 4033.

Positano: 4 Via del Saracino, tel: 089-875 067.

Amalfi: 27 Corso Repubbliche Marinare, tel: 089-871 107.

Ravello: 18bis Via Roma, tel: 089-57 096.

Capri: 1 Piazza Umberto I, Capri Town, tel: 081-837 0686; Marina Grande, tel: 081-837 0634; 59 Via G. Orlandi, Anacapri, tel: 081-837 1524.

Ischia: 72 Via Antonio Sogliuzzo, tel: 081-507 4231.

Procida: 173 Via Vittorio Emanuele, tel: 081-896 9628.

TOURS AND GUIDES

City Sightseeing open-top buses run on five lines in Naples and the surrounding area (www.napoli.city-sightseeing.it), all of which depart from Piazza Municipio. Tickets cost €22 and last for the day, allowing you to hop on and off as you please. The smaller Shuttle service (€8 daily ticket, €3 single trip, or free with Artecard) is useful for Naples' main sights, stopping off at the Duomo, M.A.D.R.E., the Museo Archeologico

and the Museo di Capodimonte, before heading back down towards the *centro storico* and Piazza Municipio. Services also run in the Sorrentine Peninsula and on the Amalfi Coast; see www.sorrento. city-sightseeing.it for details.

Context Travel offers small-group and private walking and car tours lead by art historians and archaeologists (tel: 06-9762 5204, www. contexttravel.com/naples). Options range from specialised Baroque tours to walks exploring local Christmas traditions to pizza-making workshops; prices start at €55 per person.

TRANSPORT

Arrival by Air

Naples' airport, Capodichino (tel: 848-888 777, or 081-751 5471, www. portal.gesac.it), is 7km (4 miles) from the city centre. The Alibus airport bus stops at the port and at Piazza Garibaldi train station every 20 minutes (Mon–Fri 6.30am–11.39pm, Sat–Sun 6.30am–11.50pm; €3, buy tickets on the bus; tel: 800-639 525, www.anm.it). City bus C58 stops at the train station but not the port every 30 minutes (€1.10; buy tickets at the newsagent inside Arrivals). Both services leave from outside Arrivals.

Curreri buses run to Sorrento from outside Arrivals (9am, 11am, 1pm, 2.30pm, 4.30pm and 7.30pm; €10; 1hr 15min). The same bus stops at Pompeii (same price; 25 minutes) en route.

A taxi to the port should cost about €19, to Piazza Garibaldi €15, to Vomero or hotels along the Lungomare near Chiaia €23. Check the list of fixed-price fares next to the tourist information desk. If you want to pay a fixed fare, you need to request it at the start of the journey (ask for *tariffa fissa*).

Arrival by Rail or Bus

Most trains from other parts of Italy and Europe arrive at the main station, Napoli Centrale in Piazza Garibaldi. Metro and suburban rail lines also pass through here, and outside is a terminus for city and long-distance buses. From Piazza Garibaldi, take bus 1 to the port area, metro line 2 to Montesanto or bus R2 for the *centro storico*, or metro line 2 to Amedeo or Mergellina for Chiaia.

Arrival by Boat

Frequent hydrofoils from Sorrento, the Amalfi Coast and islands arrive at Naples' port, Molo Beverello. Some services run from the islands and Pozzuoli to the smaller port of Mergellina, connected to the city by metro line 2. Larger, slower ferries from the islands arrive at Calata Porto di Massa, a 10-minute walk east of Molo Beverello. For schedules, check daily paper *Il Mattino*, or the tourist offices (see p.91).

Arrival by Road

From the UK, the usual route is through France, entering Italy at the Alps and taking the autostrada down to Naples.

Above from far left: inside Naples' Duomo; the train can be a great way to arrive in Naples.

Public Transport

The transport network within the bay area is very efficient and – with the exception of the poorly connected Campi Flegrei – all the major sites and resorts are well served by buses, trains and boats. Pompeii, Herculaneum and Vesuvius are easily reached by train on the Circumvesuviana line from Sorrento or Naples. Transport connections between the islands and coastal resorts are efficient and reasonably priced. Ask at the tourist office for the free transport map.

Tickets. UnicoCampania tickets (www.unicocampania.it) are available in various different forms covering the whole region, and are sold in *tabacchi* shops. Within Naples, you will need UnicoNapoli tickets, available as: 90-minute ticket €1.10, all-day pass €3.10, or €2.60 at weekends. The 3T tourist ticket (€20) is valid for three days for travel around the entire region, and includes the Alibus and transport on Ischia and Procida. Some versions of the Artecard *(see p.11)* allow free travel on public transport.

On board buses, stamp your ticket in the machine; on metros, it needs to be stamped at the entrance gate.

Buses. Progress through the traffic-choked streets is often painfully slow. The main intersection is Piazza Municipio (bus stop outside the Castel Nuovo) and Via San Carlo (bus stop outside Galleria Umberto I). The most useful lines are: R1 (for the Archaeological Museum and Piazza Dante), R2 (to the station), R3 (Riviera di Chiaia and Mergellina), R4 (Capodimonte).

SITA buses (www.sitabus.it) have the Sorrento peninsula and Amalfi Coast covered, with services from Naples' Molo Immacolatella in the port area. Buses from Sorrento to Positano and Amalfi depart in front of the main station (for Ravello you need to change at Amalfi). SEPSA buses serve the Naples suburbs and the Campi Flegrei. Two routes on Ischia circumnavigate the island; on Capri there are regular bus services between the major points of interest; buses on Procida link the port to the main villages.

Metros. The metro, currently being extended, can be very useful, especially Line 2, which stops at Piazza Garibaldi, Montesanto (for Via Toledo and connections to the Campi Flegrei), Piazza Amedeo (for Chiaia and the Vomero funicular), Mergellina and Pozzuoli. Line 1 runs between Piazza Dante, Museo (for the Archaeological Museum) and northeast Naples via Piazza Vanvitelli (Vomero); when complete, this line will be circular and link the city centre and the airport. Services operate 6am–11pm, with trains roughly every 7 minutes.

Funiculars. Naples' funiculars serve the Vomero district. The Funicolare

Centrale leaves from the bottom end of Via Toledo, the Funicolare di Chiaia from Piazza Amedeo and the Funicolare di Montesanto links Montesanto station to Via Morghen (nearest to the Vomero attractions).

Trains. Napoli Centrale can be a confusing place to take a train. The main train station (tel: 892 021, or 06-6847 5475 from abroad, or visit www. ferroviedellostato.it) is on the ground floor; downstairs are the metro and Circumvesuviana services (for Pompeii, Herculaneum and Sorrento; tel: 800 053 939, or 081-7722 444; www.vesuviana. it), though to catch a Circumvesuviana train (roughly every 30 minutes) it's best to go to the more orderly terminus at Porta Nolana, a few streets south.

Cumana trains (www.sepsa.it) for the Campi Flegrei depart from Montesanto station (Metro line 2) in the centre of town.

Tickets for Trenitalia trains can be bought online or by phone, and picked up from one of the self-service machines in the station, where you can also buy your tickets directly. Buy UnicoCampania tickets for Circumvesuviana and Cumana services from the ticket office at the terminus of the line or from *tabacchi* shops. The stops along the line are divided into various fare zones; a day return to Pompeii costs €4.70, to Sorrento €6.70. Tickets for all trains must be stamped before boarding at one of the yellow machines.

Ferries. There are frequent crossings between Naples, the islands and Sorrento. In summer there are services to the Amalfi Coast towns, too. Hydrofoils *(aliscafi)* depart from Molo Beverello, near Castel Nuovo, and the smaller port of Mergellina to the west. The main operators are Caremar (tel: 892-123; www.caremar.it), Snav (tel: 081-428 55 55; www.snav.it), NLG (tel: 081-552 0763; www.navlib.it), Alilauro (tel: 081-497 2222; www.alilauro.it) and LMP (tel: 081-704 1911; www.consorziolmp.it). The summer-only Metrò del Mare service (tel: 081-497 1036; www.metrodel mare.com) is cheap and frequent.

Ferries *(traghetti)* are slower, but you can sit on deck and take in the coastal scenery as you go. Caremar has the inter-island monopoly and Medmar (tel: 081-333 4411; www.medmar group.it) runs an Ischia service. All ferries leave from Calata Porta di Massa, a 10-minute walk from Molo Beverello. There are also services to Ischia and Procida from Pozzuoli.

Taxis. Meters in white taxis tend to start at around €3. Between 10pm and 7am; on Sundays; for luggage; and for airport pick-ups and drop-offs there is a surcharge. If the meter *(tassometro)* isn't switched on, point this out to the taxi driver, or agree a fixed price *(tariffa fissa)* before starting. You can order a radio taxi by phone (tel: 081-556 4444 or 081-

8888) for a supplement of around €1. Don't worry too much about tipping; most drivers will do the rounding up for you. Water taxis also operate in the coastal resorts and island ports.

Driving

Unless you want to venture off the beaten track and explore the hinterland, driving is not a sensible option for getting around: the traffic is horrendous (particularly along the Amalfi Coast in summer), parking is a problem, and if you're not used to driving in Italian cities, the general disregard for the rules of the road will do little for your stress levels. If you're determined to drive, note that Naples' *centro storico* is off-limits to non-residential vehicles at certain times of the day (look for the ZTL – *zona a traffico limitato* – signs), and that you cannot take a car on to Capri.

Car and Scooter Rental. You can rent a car at the airport, though it's a good idea to book before you arrive. Rates are usually inclusive of insurance, but check to make sure you're completely covered. Most rental companies will supply a car with a full tank.

The following companies have desks in the airport Arrivals hall: Avis (tel: 081-780 5790; www.avis. co.uk), Dollar (tel: 081-780 5702; www.dollar.com), Europcar (tel: 081-780 5643; www.europcar.co.uk), Hertz (tel: 081-780 2971; www. hertz.co.uk), Maggiore (tel: 081-780 3011; www.maggiore.com), Sixt (tel: 081-751 2055; www.sixt.co.uk).

Renting a scooter is to be avoided in Naples, but can be a fun way of getting around the islands *(see p.74 and p.78)*; on Ischia, the largest island, you may be better off with a car. In the Amalfi Coast area, try Positano Rent Scooter (tel: 089-873 399; www.positanorent scooter.com).

Parking. Street parking costs €2–€5, though in Naples supervised parking is a must. Parking lots *(parcheggio)* are marked with a blue 'P'. The most convenient is at the port, Molo Beverello (tel: 335-499 658; www.parcheggio beverello.com; open 24 hours a day). Outside Naples, make sure your hotel has parking facilities; Positano has several car parks in the upper town, but parking restrictions in Ravello and Amalfi mean you have to leave your car outside town.

V

VISAS AND PASSPORTS

EU passport-holders do not need a visa; a valid passport or ID card is sufficient. Visitors from the US, Canada, Australia and New Zealand do not require visas for stays of up to three months; non-EU citizens need a full passport.

Nationals of most other countries do need a visa. This must be obtained in advance from the Italian Consulate.

Above from far left: posing in Pompeii; ferry at Procida; a fully loaded scooter.

Petrol
Petrol stations *(benzinaio)* are usually manned – just ask *il pieno*, which means 'fill her up'. Rates vacillate around €1.50 a litre. For unleaded ask for *senza piombo*. Some stations accept credit cards, but it's a good idea to carry cash in case they don't.

Naples' fanciest hotels are concentrated on the seafront (Lungomare) around Castel dell'Ovo and in Chiaia, but for atmosphere you might prefer one of the newer boutique hotels set in historic Centro Storico *palazzi*. Budget hotels cluster around the station, but this is not Naples' nicest corner; it's worth spending more to stay in the centre. Sorrento is a good base for exploring the islands and the Amalfi Coast, and Naples is only a 40-minute boat ride or one-hour train ride away. Accommodation in the bay area is generally pricey, especially on Capri and in the main towns of the Amalfi Coast, though in the last few years the area has seen some good-value B&Bs opening, making a stay here viable for visitors on small budgets, too. Hotels get booked up well in advance, so reserve as early as possible; most hotels along the coast close between November and Easter, but may reopen for a few days over New Year.

Naples

Decumani

Via San Giovanni Maggiore Pignatelli 15; tel: 081-551 8188; www.decumani.com; €€

This self-styled 'cultural hotel' is set in the one-time residence of Cardinal Riario Sforza: an elegant high-ceilinged *palazzo* with a breakfast salon that has to be seen to be believed. The rooms are spacious and tasteful, and the location in the heart of the *centro storico* is hard to beat.

Excelsior

Via Partenope 48; tel: 081-764 0111; www.excelsior.it; €€€

The grande dame of Naples' hotels, right on the waterfront, offers old-school glamour in spades. The rooms are spacious and wonderfully opulent, and the top-floor terrace is a lovely spot for breakfast or for a sunset cocktail in the summer months, offering sweeping views of the bay.

Micalô

Riviera di Chiaia 88; tel: 081-761 7131; www.micalo.it; €€€€

Perfectly at home in chic Chiaia, this nine-room boutique hotel has a distinctly designer feel. Most of the rooms are on two levels, with stylish bathrooms up above. The acres of natural materials and modern neutrals are enhanced by an array of modern art by young Neapolitan artists on the walls. Excellent breakfasts, too.

Palazzo Decumani

Piazzetta Giustino Fortunato 8; tel: 081-420 1379; www.palazzodecumani.com; €€

Price categories (for a double room in high season including breakfast):

€€€€	over €270
€€€	€170–270
€€	€100–170
€	under €100

The sweeping spiral staircase at this boutique hotel sets the tone for the neo-Baroque decor throughout. The rooms are very comfortable, with luxuries such as plush chaises longues and marble bathrooms with Etro toiletries. The welcome cocktail is a nice touch, too.

Piazza Bellini

Via Santa Maria di Costantinopoli 101; tel: 081-451 732; www.hotel piazzabellini.com; €€

Set in a historic palazzo, this hotel has been totally revamped and now boasts a fun, modern interior. The quirky sketches of a local cartoonist enliven the white walls, and the bright, contemporary rooms really make the hotel stand out among Naples' play-it-safe options. Staff are endlessly helpful and the location is a bonus – a stone's throw from leafy Piazza Bellini.

Tribù

Via dei Tribunali 339; tel: 081-454 793; www.tribunapoli.com; €

In the heart of the *centro storico*, this small, stylish B&B is run by arty couple Gaetano and Alessandra, who are full of suggestions on how to plan your stay. Rooms are thoughtfully furnished, with interesting art and design touches, and breakfast is taken on the sunny terrace in fine weather. No credit cards.

Vesuvio

Via Partenope 45; tel: 081-764 0044; www.vesuvio.it; €€€€

With a prime position on this five-star strip, the Vesuvio stands out for its charmingly old-fashioned feel and direct views of the Castel dell'Ovo. The rooms are as luxurious as you'd expect, and breakfast is a sumptuous banquet overlooking the waters of the bay.

Sorrento

Casa Astarita

Corso Italia 67; tel: 081-877 4906; www.casastarita.com; €

Right on Sorrento's lively main drag, this family-run B&B has individually furnished rooms, each decorated with a different colour scheme. You can use the library in the shared sitting room, and the free juices and water are a nice touch. Breakfast – with homemade cakes and jams – is a highlight.

Excelsior Vittoria

Piazza Tasso 34; tel: 081-877 7111; www.excelsiorvittoria.com; €€€€

The most refined of the grand clifftop hotels, the magnificent Excelsior is separated from the riff-raff on busy Piazza Tasso by its beautiful, flower-filled gardens. There are elegant salons, terraces with stunning views of the bay, a breakfast room with a wonderful frescoed ceiling and a lovely pool surrounded by greenery. It's worth paying extra for a room with a sea view.

Ulisse Deluxe Hostel

Via del Mare 22; tel: 081-877 4753; www.ulissedeluxe.com; €

Thanks to the 'hostel' tag, Ulisse is off many tourists' radar, but banish all thoughts of dingy dormitories: a hostel in name only, this place has spacious private rooms with all mod cons, a swimming pool in the basement and a perfect location, midway between the town centre and the beach. Rooms may feel a little bland, but with rates this low, who's complaining?

Amalfi

Floridiana

Salita Brancia 1; tel: 089-873 6373; www.hotelfloridiana.it; €€

In a tranquil courtyard off Amalfi's heaving main street, this hotel has won awards for its customer service. The rooms are slightly old-fashioned in style, though none the worse for it; no. 3 is the biggest of the standard rooms, but it's worth paying the extra €10 for a bigger 'superior', or €20 for a two-level 'junior suite' with hydromassage bath.

Furore Inn

Via dell'Amore, Furore; tel: 089-830 4711; www.furoreinn.it; €€€€

This five-star hideaway in the village of Furore, just 4km (2 miles) from Amalfi but a world away from the tourist crowds, boasts stunning sea views from its rooms. There's plenty to occupy you, from lounging by the infinity pool to pampering in the spa or a meal at the superb terrace restaurant, but a courtesy shuttle to Amalfi is available if you can bear to tear yourself away.

Sant'Alfonso

Via Sant'Alfonso 6, Furore; tel: 089-830 515; www.agriturismo santalfonso.it; €

A stay in this excellent *agriturismo*, well off the tourist trail but only 8km (5 miles) from Amalfi, is a wonderfully peaceful experience. Set high up in the mountains with stunning views, this is a serene retreat with nine comfortable, cosily decorated rooms, welcoming hosts and heart-stopping views. There's a good on-site restaurant too; the food is accompanied by wine from the farm's vineyards. Resident goats and geese complete the bucolic scene.

Villa Lara

Via delle Cartiere 1; tel: 089-873 6358; www.villalara.it; €€

A lift whisks you above the lemon groves and blooming bougainvillea to this bijou seven-room retreat. The simple, tasteful rooms have brightly coloured feature walls and hydromassage showers; the 'junior suite' is a calm, all-white oasis set under the eaves. Breakfast is served on the mini-terrace between two sheer cliff faces, with wonderful views.

Price categories (for a double room in high season including breakfast):	
€€€€	over €270
€€€	€170–270
€€	€100–170
€	under €100

Above from far left: outdoor dining options at the Excelsior Vittoria; elegant decor at the Decumani.

Positano

Buca di Bacco

Via Rampa Teglia 4; tel: 089-875 699; www.bucadibacco.it; €€€€

With an excellent beachside location, acres of majolica tiles and antique furnishings, the Buca di Bacco has long been one of Positano's most desirable hotels. The rooms are traditionally furnished, though pale shades and French windows leading to sea-view balconies (in most rooms) give them a breezy feel. The hotel doesn't have claim to a section of beach, though a solarium is available for sun-worshippers.

Palazzo Murat

Via dei Mulini 23; tel: 089-875 177; www.palazzomurat.it; €€€

With an impressive historic pedigree – this was the home of Napoleon's brother-in-law Joachim Murat, who was also King of Naples – this beautiful hotel has been run by the same family for generations. Heirlooms and cool tiled floors set the tone; request a room in the older, more charming main part of the hotel. The lovely central courtyard, nestled among palm trees, trailing bougainvillea and other Mediterranean blooms, makes a lovely spot for breakfast, and for candlelit dinners.

Palazzo Talamo

Via Pasitea 117; tel: 089-875 562; www.palazzotalamo.it; €€

Eleven fresh, bright rooms are painted in restful pastel hues that take their cue from the traditional majolica floor tiles. All have sea views and private terraces; those on floor minus-2 are the best. Family-run, the service is excellent, and there are several very good restaurants along this stretch, too.

Pensione Maria Luisa

Via Fornillo 42; tel: 089-812 2360; www.pensionemarialuisa.com; €

Run by the ever-enthusiastic Carlo, this budget hotel has a friendly, welcoming feel. It's tucked away in a warren of whitewashed alleys in the Fornillo district – so walking back from the beach involves a slog up steep flights of steps. All of the rooms are pleasant and spotless, but it's definitely worth paying the extra €10 for one of the rooms with a huge sea-view terrace. Unusually, it's open all year. No credit cards.

Ravello

Caruso

Piazza San Giovanni del Toro 2; tel: 089-858 801; www.hotelcaruso.com; €€€€

An extensive renovation transformed this formerly crumbling 11th-century *palazzo* into an incredible destination hotel – one of the finest on the Amalfi Coast. The rooms are sumptuous, the infinity pool dazzling, the views breathtaking, but it's the details that matter: aromatic herbs grown in the garden go into making the mini-masterpieces served up in the Belvedere restaurant, the opulent marble bathrooms come

complete with Bulgari toiletries; and there are complimentary boat trips along the coast.

Parsifal

Via Gioacchino D'Anna 5; tel: 089-857 144; www.hotelparsifal.com; €€

This charming small hotel, half of which was recently renovated, has been run by the welcoming Mansi family for years. Dotted with antiques, it has a pleasantly old-fashioned feel, and the terrace courtyard, with superb views of the sea below, is a plus. There's a restaurant; half-board is available on request.

Villa Porta Donica

Via della Repubblica 46; www.porta donica.it; €€€

This stunning villa, hidden down a flight of steps a 15-minute walk from Ravello's main piazza, is a real find: five beautiful rooms, gardens swathed in luxuriant bougainvillea and a swimming pool – all with unrivalled sea views. Though generally only available for weekly rentals in the summer, three-night rentals are possible out of season.

Capri

JK Capri

Via Prov. Marina Grande 225; tel: 081-838 4001; www.jkcapri.com; €€€€

When Capri's narrow streets are crammed with day-trippers, retreat to this five-star bolthole, whose breezy, vaguely nautical decor is enlivened with quirky antiques and perfumed with the scent of freshly cut blooms. With four-posters in the rooms, balconies suspended over the sea and spectacular views, waking up here is a treat. And you'll have almost as much fun hanging out on the huge wraparound terrace, lounging by the infinity pool or being pampered in the spa.

La Tosca

Via Dalmazio Birago 5; tel: 081-837 0989; email: h.tosca@capri.it; €

With just 10 rooms, this family-run one-star place a five-minute walk from the Piazzetta is a real find in Capri – early booking is a must. Among the spotless white rooms, no. 47 is the best, with its own sunny terrace offering lovely views over San Giacomo and the hillside. All rooms have air-conditioning and Wi-fi – a bonus in this price bracket. The management is very helpful, too.

La Minerva

Via Occhio Marino 8; tel: 081-837 7067; www.laminervacapri.com; €€€

This boutique four-star hotel has 18 rooms, all beautifully furnished, with high, cross-vaulted ceilings and tradi-

Price categories (for a double room in high season including breakfast):

€€€€	over €270
€€€	€170–270
€€	€100–170
€	under €100

tional ceramic-tiled floors; ask for no. 43, with its jacuzzi and large balcony offering spellbinding views. The pool is set among fragrant mimosa, almond and citrus trees, and breakfast is served on the rooftop terrace in fine weather, with more views to swoon over.

Ischia

Albergo Il Monastero
Castello Aragonese, Ischia Ponte; tel: 081-992 435; www.albergoil monastero.it; €€

This hotel enjoys a fantastic location, high up in the Castello Aragonese, and the views from this lofty perch are predictably dazzling. Having access to the castle after dark, once the day-trippers have gone home, is quite a thrill. When you're not roaming the battlements, you can visit the monastery's own terraced gardens, bursting with fruit and vegetables used by the hotel restaurant, as well as grapes that go into making its own white wine. The rooms themselves are simply but attractively furnished.

Albergo della Regina Isabella
Piazza Santa Restituta 1, Lacco Ameno; tel: 081-994 322; www. reginaisabella.it; €€€€

One of the island's most upscale choices, the Regina Isabella is glamorous, but far from snooty: perfectly coiffed *signore* are happy to be seen in their dressing gowns at breakfast, and the staff are endlessly helpful and welcoming. Some of the rooms have been

given a modern makeover, but most are classic and old-fashioned – and some are very large. The spa is highly regarded, but is more for targeted therapies than indulgent pampering; the restaurant is excellent. Check the website for bargain low-season deals.

Il Moresco
Via E. Gianturco 16, Ischia Porto; tel: 081-981 355; www.ilmoresco.it; €€

In the centre of Ischia Porto and just steps from its own private beach, this hotel is an excellent base for exploring Ischia. The decor is quite traditional in feel, and a certain old-world charm pervades: you can have aperitifs in the piano bar before moving through to the restaurant, where the dapper waiters are a paragon of old-fashioned service. The on-site spa has three pools and a raft of treatments. Half-board is usual in high season – and as the restaurant is excellent, this is no hardship.

Procida

La Casa Sul Mare
Via Salita Castello 13; tel: 081-896 8799; www.lacasasulmare.it; €€

Procida's top choice is this enchanting hotel, set in a lovely 18th-century *palazzo*. Rooms are bright and simply furnished in aquatic shades, with balconies overlooking the sea and the picture-perfect fishing village of Corricella below. Breakfast is served in the garden to the sound of the sea, and includes delicious home-made cakes.

In Naples the best fish restaurants and more up-market establishments with bay views are found in the Borgo Marinaro area, and in Santa Lucia, Mergellina and further west in Posillipo. For family-run trattorias, authentic pizzerias and cheaper food in general, head for the *centro storico*, where the exuberant atmosphere makes any meal memorable – even if it's just a slice of takeaway pizza.

In the more touristic coastal resorts, as a general rule restaurants in the main piazza or on the waterfront will be more expensive; for a more authentic experience, head off the tourist trail.

Eating out is central to Italian culture, and a slap-up dinner on Saturday or lunch on Sunday is a time-honoured ritual; in view of this, booking ahead is always a good idea, particularly in high season.

Naples

Antica Latteria
Vico Alarbardieri 30; tel: 081-012 8775; Mon–Sat L&D, Sun L; €€

Just off lively Piazza dei Martiri, this bustling, cheerful place takes its name from its origins as a dairy, and the simple, *osteria*-style decor and wood-beamed ceiling retain the old-fashioned feel. The honestly priced dishes are excellent value in this part of town: a succulent *tagliata* steak on a bed of rocket will set you back just €12.

Da Michele
Via Cesare Sersale 1-7; tel: 081-553 9204; www.damichele.net; Mon–Sat 10am–11pm; €

In business for 140 years and still going strong, this venerable pizzeria only serves two types of pizza – the classic *margherita* and the *marinara* (with a topping of tomato, garlic, oregano and olive oil) – but they are king-size and near-perfect. The decor is minimalist in the extreme – simple marble-topped tables and a vast pizza oven take up most of the space – but it has a legion of fans. Be prepared to queue.

Fantasia Gelati
Piazza Vanvitelli 22; tel: 081-578 8383; daily 7am–1am; €

There are always hordes of people devouring ice creams on the pavement outside this excellent *gelateria* in Vomero's lively main piazza, and a permanent queue inside – which at least gives you time to choose which of the 50-plus flavours to go for.

Friggitoria Vomero
Via Cimarosa 44; tel: 081-578 3130; Mon–Fri 9.30am–2.30pm and

Two-course meal for one with a glass of house wine:

€€€€	Over €40
€€€	€26–40
€€	€16–25
€	Under €15

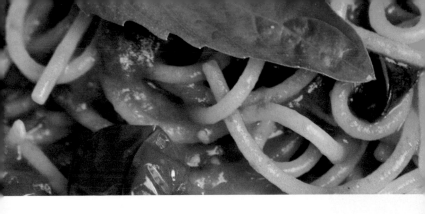

5–9.30pm, Sat 9.30am–2.30pm and 5–10.30pm; €

This Vomero institution is a great place for lunch on the run, offering fried specialities such as slices of battered aubergine, incredibly good value at just €0.20. There are sweet treats too – try the *graffe*, sugar-coated Neapolitan doughnuts. It's takeaway only – enjoy your picnic in the tranquil Villa Floridiana, a short stroll away.

Gran Caffè La Caffettiera

Piazza dei Martiri 26; tel: 081-764 4243; www.grancaffelacaffettiera. com; Mon–Fri 7am–10.30pm, Sat 7am–midnight, Sun 7am–11pm; €

This local favourite, in Chiaia's main square, is busy throughout the day: Gucci-clad *signorine* perch on the high bar stools to sip a morning *macchiato*, office suits pop in for a panino or a sugar-dusted pastry, and a dressed-up evening crowd gossips over *aperitivi* on the decked terrace.

La Locanda del Grifo

Via F. Del Giudice 14; tel: 081-442 0815; www.lalocandadelgrifo.com; daily 1–4pm, 7pm–midnight; €

This pizzeria-restaurant enjoys an atmospheric location, with outdoor tables on a pretty *centro storico* square just off hectic Via dei Tribunali. The huge pizzas are the draw here, but the menu also offers a handful of mainly fish-based *secondi*. Look out for the

griffin that gives the restaurant its name, perched on the campanile opposite.

L.U.I.S.E

Piazza dei Martiri 68; tel: 081-415 367; Mon–Sat 8am–8.30pm, Sun 8am–3pm; €

This always-busy *tavola calda* has hot and cold dishes to take away, ranging from generous hunks of *torta rustica* (quiche-like tarts) to pasta salads and savoury pastries stuffed with spinach and cheese. Everything is of an excellent quality, and the low prices make it a perfect spot for a quick lunch; there are a few seats if you want to eat in, too. There's a second branch at Via Toledo 266–268.

Mattozzi

Via Finangieri 16; tel: 081-416 378; Mon–Sat L&D; €€

Give your credit card a rest after a shopping trip in Chiaia at this reasonably priced pizzeria. You'll have to get here early to nab one of the hotly contested outdoor tables on the vine-clad terrace, as no bookings are taken. Mattozzi is renowned for its deliciously crispy pizza, cooked in a wood-fired oven, but meat and fish dishes are also served.

Mimi alla Ferrovia

Via Alfonso d'Aragona 21; tel: 081-553 8525; Mon–Sat 9am–midnight; €€

In business for 70 years and still a bastion of old-fashioned service, this

Above from far left: the Borgo Marinaro has restaurants aplenty; you won't go short of pasta in Naples.

traditional trattoria is an unlikely survivor in the culinary wasteland around the central station – great if you have a train to catch. Downstairs is buzzy at lunch, while the more elegant first floor is more atmospheric at dinner.

Taverna dell'Arte

Rampe S. Giovanni Maggiore 1A; tel: 081-552 7558; www.tavernadellarte.it; Mon–Sat 12.30–3.30pm, 8–10.30pm; €€€

Hidden away on a side street near Via Mezzocannone, this is many people's idea of the perfect little Italian trattoria: terracotta-tiled floors, walls lined with wine bottles and simple white linen on the tables; four tables sit under a flower-strewn bower outside. Simple, well-executed dishes include meatballs with local greens and home-made soups (no pizza).

Un SorRiso Integrale

Vico S. Pietro a Maiella 6; tel: 081-455 026; www.sorrisointegrale.com; daily 12.30–3.45pm, 7.15pm–midnight; €€

The perfect antidote to pizza and pasta overload, this organic vegetarian restaurant-cum-health food store is in a small courtyard off Piazza Bellini. With fresh flowers on communal wooden tables and crates of fresh produce dotted around, it has an appealingly homespun feel, and the food's good, too: big salads, soups, cheese plates and home-made cakes. The *piatto unico*, a selection of the day's specials, costs €9.

Pompeii

Il Principe

Piazza Bartolo Longo 8; tel: 081-850 5566; www.ilprincipe.com; €€€

If you haven't packed a picnic for Pompeii and fancy a splurge, this prestigious restaurant is the place. The regional dishes are excellent, but the special menu of contemporary dishes inspired by ancient Roman recipes is what really sets it apart. You need to call first to request this, but the speciality *cassata di Oplontis*, a delectable ricotta cheesecake sweetened with honey and studded with candied fruits, is always on the menu.

Sorrento and the Peninsula

Da Franco

Corso Italia 265, Sorrento; tel: 081-877 2066; daily 8am–2am; €

This rowdy locals' pizzeria is at Corso Italia's non-touristic end. Take a seat at one of the communal wooden tables and watch your pizza being prepared by one of the expert *pizzaioli* in the open kitchen. The house special is topped with tomato, cheese, rocket and parmesan, but there are plenty of other options to tempt you, too.

Two-course meal for one with a glass of house wine:

€€€€	Over €40
€€€	€26–40
€€	€16–25
€	Under €15

Above from far left: inside Naples' Caffè Gambrinus; an Ischia restaurant; pizza is the Naples staple.

La Conca del Sogno

Via San Marciano 9, Nerano; tel: 081-808 1036; www.concadel sogno.it; €€€

Finding this tucked-away restaurant is not easy, but worth the effort. As you drive down towards Marine del Cantone, after Nerano follow signs to the Villaggio Syrenuse. Ask for permission to drive through this campsite, beyond which the road cuts through a ravine and opens out on to a tiny beach and the lovely Conca del Sogno – an excellent restaurant that also has six rooms. Call if you want their shuttle boat to pick you up from Marina del Cantone.

Sant'Antonino

Via Santa Maria delle Grazie 6, Sorrento; tel: 081-877 1200; daily noon–4pm, 7pm–1am; €€

Right in the centre of Sorrento but tucked away in an elevated position up a flight of steps, this restaurant is a hit with locals and tourists alike for its delicious food and jovial service. There are no bay views, but dining on a terrace full of citrus trees makes up for it; look out for the hybrid that grows both oranges and lemons.

Taverna del Capitano

Piazza delle Sirene 10–11, Marina del Cantone; tel: 081-808 1028; www.tavernadelcapitano.com; daily noon–2.30pm, 7–10.30pm; closed Jan, Feb and Mon in winter; €€€€

Marina del Cantone is renowned for its fish restaurants, and this is one of the best. With two Michelin stars and a stellar reputation, it invites high expectations, and the superb fish dishes don't disappoint. The dining room is lined with inlaid wood, and the wine cellar, set in the cherry-wood hull of a reproduction Sorrentine ship, is fabulous.

The Amalfi Coast

Da Gemma

Via Fra Gerardo Sasso 11, Amalfi; tel: 089-871 345; www.trattoriada gemma.com; Mar–Sept Thur–Tue 12.30–2.30pm, 7.30–11.30pm; €€€€

This landmark trattoria, in business since 1872, is famous for its fish soup and its surprisingly delicious aubergine-and-chocolate dessert, but there are many standout dishes: try the catch of the day baked in a salt crust, or the citrus-marinated tuna carpaccio. Whether you eat inside in the spacious, airy dining room or on the elegant roof terrace with views of the Duomo, booking is essential.

Da Vincenzo

Viale Pasitea 172-178, Positano; tel: 089-875 128; Mar–Oct daily 1–3pm, 7–11.30pm, closed Tue lunch end June–Oct; €€€

This family-run restaurant is not the cheapest in town, but worth the splurge for the outstanding cooking and local delicacies that you'll only find here: a typical starter might be

totani e patate – squid cooked with potatoes – followed by a main of sea bream flavoured with lemon and orange peel and baked in a bread crust. Neapolitan music in the evening adds to the buzzy atmosphere.

Dolceria dell'Antico Porto

Supportico Rua, Amalfi; tel: 089-871 143; www.dolceria-amalfi.com; Tue–Sun 8.30am–9pm; €

This boutique *pasticceria* in the heart of Amalfi is an essential stop for foodies. The owner, Tiziano Mita, is a whiz with pastry, taking the long-established Neapolitan tradition to new heights; his *sfogliatella* is given a new twist in the shape of a *trullo* – the typical Puglian conical-roofed house – while the traditional *delizia* lemon-cream cake is paired with an olive-oil biscuit. Melt-in-the-mouth lemon and almond pastries are another speciality.

Donna Rosa

Via Montepertuso 97–99, Montepertuso; tel: 089-811 806; Wed–Mon 11am–3pm, 6–10pm; €€€€

Just above Positano, the quieter, more workaday village of Montepertuso harbours several very good restaurants, but Donna Rosa is the standout choice, and is packed with dressed-up locals every night. The expertly prepared seafood is the main draw, although the stunning views come a close second. Leave room for dessert – the hot chocolate soufflé is to die for. Booking essential.

Rosselinis

Hotel Palazzo Sasso, Via San Giovanni del Toro 28, Ravello; tel: 089-818 181; www.palazzosasso.com; Apr–Oct 7.30–9pm; €€€€

In the opulent surroundings of the Hotel Palazzo Sasso, this two-Michelin-starred restaurant has a splendid setting, its terrace perched high above the bobbing lights of the fishing boats below. Chef Pino Lavarra trained under Raymond Blanc, and the food is suitably high-class: a highlight of the tasting menu is lamb fillet in a rose crust with white asparagus, in an anchovy and sun-dried tomato sauce.

The Islands

Aurora

Via Fuorlovado 18, Capri; tel: 081-837 0181; www.auroracapri.com; daily noon–4pm, 7pm–midnight; €€€€

This is one of Capri's smartest restaurants, with dishes such as fish carpaccio with vanilla salt and pine nuts, and linguine with lobster and asparagus, though (pricey) pizzas are on offer, too. The elegant terrace dotted with pots of fragrant blooms

Two-course meal for one with a glass of house wine:	
€€€€	Over €40
€€€	€26–40
€€	€16–25
€	Under €15

is right on Capri's main shopping strip, making it prime people-watching territory – but booking for dinner rather than lunch will make for a more tranquil experience.

Calise Caffè Concerto
Piazza degli Eroi, Ischia Porto, Ischia; tel: 081-991 270; daily 7.30am–1.30am; €

An Ischian institution, this vast place is a bar, *pasticceria* and pizzeria in one, and even a club in the summer months, with live music nightly. Its lushly planted gardens make a great place for an *aperitivo*, and if the chattering crowds get too much, there are plenty of little hidden corners to retreat to.

Da Alberto
Via Roma 9–11, Capri; tel: 081-837 0622; daily 5.30am–midnight, Nov–Mar closed Tue, Aug open 24 hours; €

In business since 1946, Da Alberto is a good spot for a coffee and a wedge of *torta caprese* – Capri's deliciously moist almond-and-chocolate namesake. In August, the bar is famous for its *cornetto caldi* (hot-from-the-oven croissants), served all night long to bleary-eyed bar-hoppers.

La Conchiglia
Chiaia beach, Procida; tel: 081-896 7602; www.laconchigliaristorante. com; daily 1–3.30pm, 8–10.30pm; €€

Right on Chiaia beach, La Conchiglia is a wonderful place for a family lunch (this is one of the safer beaches for children) or a romantic dinner, with views to swoon over. Pasta with mussels and courgettes is a speciality *primo*, and the grilled fish is superb. No road access; take a taxi boat from Corricella or walk down the steps from Via Pizzaco.

La Savardina da Edoardo
Via Lo Capo 8, Capri; tel: 081-837 6300; daily noon–3pm, 7–11pm, closed Tue in winter; €€€

In a nondescript alley on the way up to Villa Jovis, but well signposted, this rustic restaurant has a lovely shady terrace where you can sample traditional food beneath a canopy of orange and lemon trees. Fried courgette blossoms and sage leaves make a moreish starter; follow with the *linguine al limone*, in a creamy, zesty sauce.

Neptunus
Via Chiaia di Rose, Sant'Angelo, Ischia; tel: 081-999 702; www. ristoranteneptunus.com; mid-Mar–Dec daily 11am–3.30pm, 7pm–1am; €€€

Perched on a cliff and enjoying spectacular views, this colourful restaurant has a vibrant atmosphere in the evenings, when there's live musical entertainment. Its fresh-off-the-boat fish, expertly prepared, attracts the great and the good and photographs of VIP visitors are proudly displayed.

Above from far left: the region's climate is perfect for alfresco dining; Capri café; basket of fresh lemons.

CREDITS

Insight Step by Step
Naples & the Amalfi Coast
Written by: Natasha Foges and Cathy Muscat
Series Editor: Clare Peel
Editor: Tom Stainer
Map Production: APA Cartography Department
Picture Manager: Steven Lawrence
Art Editor: Richard Cooke
Photography: All Pictures APA/Greg Gladman except: Alamy 21T, 21B/MT, 24M, 25B, 34B, 72–3, 73B; Corbis 47B; Pietro Crincoli 64T; Courtesy Excelsior Vittoria 97T, 98TL, 98–9, 100–1; Courtesy Hotel Decumani 99TR; Courtesy Hotel Vesuvio 97T; iStockphoto 4MT, 58–9, 58TR, 84BR; Mary Evans Picture Library 25T; Pictures Colour Library 84TL; Scala Archives 46TL, 46–7, 59TL; Sibeaster 45TR; Courtesy Starwood Hotels 84BL, 96T; Lane Wilkinson Photography 20TL.
Front cover: main image: 4Corners Images; bottom left and right: iStockphoto.
Printed by: CTPS-China.

© 2011 APA Publications GmbH & Co. Verlag KG (Singapore branch)
All rights reserved

First Edition 2011

No part of this book may be reproduced, stored in a retrieval system or transmitted in any form or by any means (electronic, mechanical, photocopying, recording or otherwise), without prior written permission of APA Publications. Brief text quotations with use of photographs are exempted for book review purposes only. Information has been obtained from sources believed to be reliable, but its accuracy and completeness, and the opinions based thereon, are not guaranteed.

Although Insight Guides and the authors of this book have taken all reasonable care in preparing it, we make no warranty about the accuracy or completeness of its content, and, to the maximum extent permitted, disclaim all liability arising from its use.

CONTACTING THE EDITORS

We would appreciate it if readers would alert us to errors or outdated information by writing to us at insight@apaguide.co.uk or APA Publications, PO Box 7910, London SE1 1WE, UK.

www.insightguides.com

DISTRIBUTION

Worldwide
APA Publications GmbH & Co. Verlag KG
(Singapore branch)
7030 Ang Mo Kio Ave 5
08-65 Northstar @ AMK
Singapore 569880
Tel: (65) 570 1051
E-mail: apasin@singnet.com.sg

UK and Ireland
GeoCenter International Ltd
Meridian House, Churchill Way West
Basingstoke, Hampshire, RG21 6YR
Tel: (44) 01256 817 987
E-mail: sales@geocenter.co.uk

US
Ingram Publisher Services
One Ingram Blvd, PO Box 3006
La Vergne, TN 37086-1986
Email: customer.service@ingrampublisher
services.com

Australia
Universal Publishers
1 Waterloo Road, Macquarie Park, NSW 2113
Tel: (61) 2 9857 3700
E-mail: sales@universalpublishers.com.au

New Zealand
Hema Maps New Zealand Ltd (HNZ)
Unit 2, 10 Cryers Road
East Tamaki, Auckland 2013
Tel: (64) 9 273 6459
E-mail: sales.hema@clear.net.nz

INDEX